Silvia Guerini is a radical ecologist of Resistenze al Nanomondo, editor of the newspaper *L'Urlo della Terra* and one of the founders of FINAARGIT (International feminist network against all artificial reproduction, gender ideology and transhumanism). In the early 2000s, she was one of the founders of the Coalizione Contro Ogni Nocività (Coalition Against Every Harm) which launched a mobilisation campaign against the entry of GMOs into Europe and later a campaign against nanotechnologies. Silvia is a contributor to *Per l'abolizione della maternità surrogata* (*Towards the Abolition of Surrogate Motherhood*). The first Italian edition of this book, *Dal corpo neutro al cyborg postumano: Riflessioni critiche all'ideologia gender*, was published in 2022, the updated and extended second edition in 2023.

Other books by Silvia Guerini

*Dal corpo neutro al cyborg postumano:
Riflessioni critiche all'ideologia gender* (2022)

5G: Rete della società cibernetica
(co-author Ragusa Costantino) (2021)

*Dalla riproduzione artificiale animale alla
riproduzione artificiale umana: Transumanesimo
e produzione del vivente* (Ed.) (2020)

From the 'Neutral' Body to the Posthuman Cyborg:
A Critique of Gender Ideology

Silvia Guerini

We respectfully acknowledge the wisdom of Aboriginal and Torres Strait Islander peoples and their custodianship of the lands and waterways. The Countries on which Spinifex offices are situated are Djiru, Bunurong and Wurundjeri, Wadawurrung, Gundungarra and Noongar.

First published by Spinifex Press, 2023

Spinifex Press Pty Ltd
PO Box 200, Little River, VIC 3211, Australia
PO Box 105, Mission Beach, QLD 4852, Australia

women@spinifexpress.com.au
www.spinifexpress.com.au

Copyright © Silvia Guerini, 2023

Copyright © Elisa Boscarol, 2023: Chapters 8, 9, 10 and 11
Original English translation by Miguel Martinez; revised translation by Pauline Hopkins, Renate Klein and Susan Hawthorne

The moral right of the author has been asserted.

All rights reserved. Without limiting the rights under copyright reserved above, no part of this publication may be reproduced, stored in or introduced into a retrieval system, or transmitted, in any form or by any means (electronic, mechanical, photocopying, recording or otherwise) without prior written permission of both the copyright owner and the above publisher of the book.

Copying for educational purposes
Information in this book may be reproduced in whole or part for study or training purposes, subject to acknowledgement of the source and providing no commercial usage or sale of material occurs. Where copies of part or whole of the book are made under part VB of the *Copyright Act*, the law requires that prescribed procedures be followed. For information contact the Copyright Agency Limited.

Edited by Renate Klein, Pauline Hopkins and Susan Hawthorne
Cover Image by Estelle Disch
Cover design by Deb Snibson
Typesetting by Helen Christie, Blue Wren Books
Typeset in Minion Pro
Printed and bound in Australia by Pegasus Media & Logistics

 A catalogue record for this book is available from the National Library of Australia

ISBN: 9781925950885 (paperback)
ISBN: 9781925950892 (ebook)

Dedication

I thank Jennifer Bilek for giving me the courage to go all the way in my thinking, and Janice Raymond, from whom many reflections I cover in this book originated. And I thank both of them for allowing me to quote from their work. And I thank Elisa Boscarol for her important contribution to this topic including the chapters in this book and the creation of her television channel *Il Mondo Nuovo 2.0*.

Contents

Introduction	1
1. Sex Is Not Gender	4
2. 'Gender Identity'	9
3. Women's Prisons in California and Canada	15
4. Gender 'Neutral' Ideology in Schools	18
5. In Europe: The Matić Report	23
6. France and Spain: Significant New Legislative Steps	26
7. Steps Forward in Italy	36
8. Where Are We in Italy?	43
9. Unicorns and Inclusivity: How Gender Ideology Enters Italian Schools	46
10. Child Transitions in Italy: The 'Debate' on Puberty Blockers	51
11. Dissenting Voices: The Italian Opposition to Gender Ideology	56
12. The Tavistock and Portman Foundation: Its History at the Intersection of Psychiatry, Eugenics and Cybernetics	62
13. Trans Industry Attacking the Little Ones	66
14. The Transition of the Tavistock	80

15. We Were Wrong	84
16. An Experiment on Girls and Boys: The Consequences of Puberty Blockers and Cross-sex Hormones	90
17. No Girl or Boy is 'Born in the Wrong Body'	93
18. A Broader Reflection on Transsexualism, Transition Pathways, and Their Rise	97
19. Not Wanting to Be a Woman: The Link between Anorexia and Trans-Identification	105
20. Gender Ideology and Paedophilia	111
21. Who Funds the LGBTQ+ Movement?	118
22. From the Laboratory to Queer Cyborg Activism	132
23. The New Transhumanism and Posthuman Humanity	144

Introduction

Modern society is undergoing massive change, with new definitions of humanity emerging that are upending fundamental principles about who we are. Piecing together the forces behind these changes, the common thread that unites the drive for new definitions of, above all, women, is the *transeugenics* vision of technocrats who are striving to dictate, dominate and control world agendas.

Internationally, we are seeing a media saturation of trans and LGBTQ+ claims, but are these claims really arising from the issue of 'rights' for a very small section of the population or is there a broader and deeper agenda?

Many LGB associations and groups added TQ+ around the same time in the early 2000s. Why was it added? Why was a disassociation from embodied sex added to the LGB movement, which is based on embodied same-sex attraction?

What does it mean to claim the right to 'gender identity'? What are the consequences of introducing the concept of 'gender identity' and 'gender self-ID'?

What are the consequences of claiming that sex is *assigned* at birth?

All these delusions lead to the erasure of the material dimension of bodies and sexual difference, including erasing women, dispossessing them of their capacity to procreate if they so desire; occupying their spaces; speeding up transitions to block puberty for girls/children in ever younger age brackets; reinforcing gender stereotypes to penetrate gender neutral ideology in schools with unicorns and neutral pronouns; legalising rent-a-womb (surrogacy), extending medically assisted procreation (MAP) for all; erasing the mother, the one from whom we all come into the world, by stating that one can be born from two fathers or two mothers; and to make procreation artificial with transhuman pregnancies and artificial wombs.

In this short book I will highlight the common thread that unites TQ+ claims[1] — claims that have also gained ground in some feminist contexts — that have re-signified and transfigured feminism into so-called 'trans'feminism, gender ideology and 'transhumanism', where they overlap. I explain why I believe that 'transhumanism', queer and gender ideology lead to a 'transhumanist' and 'transeugenicist' society.

Women and women's bodies have become the terrain of appropriation and confrontation, but in this terrain I want to yield

---

1   When I refer to the LGBTQ+ movement, I am referring to the enforced joining together of two completely different groups with opposing objectives. As a result of the appropriation of the LGB community by the TQ+, there are now LGB Alliance groups in many countries speaking out about the TQ+ ideology. Feminists and LGB people have overlaps in political objectives, because they are about liberation and a political strategy that recognises power imbalances.

nothing, for what is at stake is an anthropological and ontological mutation of the human being.

The 'neutral' body of those who claim to be progressive does not consider nature. On the contrary, it actually prepares the way for the construction of the posthuman cyborg. These are the necessary ontological preliminaries to succeed in building the bodies with which to mass-produce dehumanised humans—humanoids characterised by identities and supports produced by others.[2]

---

2   Michel Onfray. *Théorie de la dictature*. Paris: Robert Laffont. 2019.

Chapter 1

Sex Is Not Gender

For postmodernists, sex is a *performance*—as Judith Butler writes—and the word acquires more meaning than material reality. Stating that "sex, by definition, will be shown to have been gender all along"[3] erases the material and corporeal dimensions. But sex exists *before* symbolism, exists before discourse and outside of it, and discourse is always only around and on the surface unlike the processes of the techno-scientific system, which penetrate bodies of the living. Sex, like any material dimension, is not reducible to the discourse around it, but it exists and cannot be denied. It will always resurface:

> 'Gender' has taken on for postmodernists the meaning of the irrelevance of sex, along with the entire material world [...] Gender has become something internal, it is no longer imposed by society as in the analyses of feminists. We are in the midst of neoliberal individualization processes. The feminist definition of gender was social and political, concerning the power relations between the two sexes, but now it is being replaced by an individualized definition,

---

3 Judith Butler. *Gender Trouble: Feminism and the Subversion of Identity*. London and New York: Routledge. 1990. <https://genius.com/Judith-butler-gender-trouble-chapter-1-subjects-of-sex-gender-desire-i-iii-annotated>, accessed 28 May 2023.

which trivializes the social forces at work by reducing gender to gender expression, that is, to the individual's choice whether to appear more or less masculine or more or less feminine.[4]

We are witnessing a postmodern erasure and deconstruction of sexual difference and bodies. But life is *sexed*—there is no possible life in the absence of sexual difference. One is born sexed before any other relationship in which a symbolic meaning, a discourse, a social element emerge. The body has a reality that thought cannot alter; in the human species, as in other mammals, there are two sexes, not a continuum:

> If endocrine disruptors can disrupt the endocrine glands, which is completely indisputable, it is evidently because a body is not only a cultural exhibit sculpted by various stereotypes but also flesh imbued with hormones in more or less variable quantities.[5]

Sex is part of what is observable, it makes no sense to say that sex is *assigned* at birth, it would be like saying that eye colour and skin colour are assigned at birth. But in a post-truth world, we should not be surprised by this either. The foundations are being laid for the disintegration of what were once considered trivial truths, recognisable through simple observations, whereas today everything becomes relative and questionable. Every dimension of existence has to pass through techno-medical criteria and through a cybernetic and transhumanist ideology. These criteria

---

[4] Daniela Danna. *Sesso e genere*. Trieste: Asterios. No. 11, Volantini Militanti. 2019.

[5] Michel Onfray. Op.cit. see Footnote 2.

and this ideology will define life, death, health, disease. And they will also define sex and so-called gender identity. Having handed the fate of existence into the hands of technicians, it is they who will decree what will be seen as the right direction.

The words 'woman' and 'man' have very clear biological meanings that do not fit into postmodern deconstruction. They do not refer to social categories, but to the flesh of bodies. Trying to change that meaning not only erases female sexed reality and some of the tools we use to study that reality, but also a history of centuries that has based women's oppression on that very sexed body. To say that a woman is an adult human female is a biological fact and has nothing to do with an alleged determinist view that human behaviour and personal qualities are purely determined by biology.

We do not *have* a body, we *are* our body and many of our experiences originate from that very body. The corporeality from which meanings start and to which they return is an ancestral dimension of being in the world:

> The meanings we create or learn do not exist only in our heads, in ineffable ideas. Our meanings also exist in our bodies—what we are, what we do, what we physically feel, what we physically know; and there is no personal psychology that is separate from what the body has learned about life.[6]

---

6   Andrea Dworkin. *Intercourse*. New York: The Free Press. 1987. Passage reproduced in *New Yorker*. 1 April 2019. <https://www.newyorker.com/magazine/2019/04/01/the-radical-style-of-andrea-dworkin#:~:text=The%20meanings%20we%20create%20or,body%20has%20learned%20about%20life>.

Menstruation for a girl is a biological and historical event around which a certain set of very different, but also very similar, collective female experiences are grouped. Men do not have experiences of menstruation, nor a history that is tied to it. Girls and women are also our bleeding, our sex, our biological rhythm:

> The body in [some] contemporary feminist theory ceases to be a robust material place, but is transformed into a fluid place of contingency that can be redefined by each person for himself or herself. […] The physical substance of the body seems to be lost in its multiple representations.[7]

Too many things blur, become undefined. Instead, let us keep those lines between organic/inorganic, flesh/metal, nervous systems/electronic circuits, life/death, nature/artificial nice and clear. Artificial wombs and *transhuman* pregnancies can never erase the difference of the sexes around procreation—a man cannot give birth and this is a bodily and substantive difference; men can only try to appropriate this experience.

Here is the post-gender and post-human world that is already present: the British Medical Association redefines the term 'woman' as 'people with a front hole'. The North American Association of Midwives recommends replacing the expressions 'caesarean section' with 'window-birth', 'expectant mothers' or 'woman giving birth' with 'person giving birth', and 'breastfeeding' with 'chestfeeding', as these earlier words might offend and

---

7   Game Over. Il corpo nello specchio delle nuove tecnologie. 2016. <https://www.resistenzealnanomondo.org/necrotecnologie/il-corpo-di-genere-nello-specchio-delle-nuove-tecnologie-game-over/>, accessed 9 October 2021.

discriminate against transgender people. These are not mere linguistic acrobatics; this is a deliberate process that erases the procreation dimension and the sexuality dimension of the female body.

To conclude, one cannot change sex, one can only change gender, one's outward representation. These representations of woman are also taken to the extreme, with their reliance on, and reinforcement of, female stereotypes, with a fetishisation of what are socially regarded as female behaviours and dress, and an objectification and fetishisation of a woman's body. But a 'transwoman' is a man and always will be, regardless of hormones, surgical butchery, cosmetic surgeries: *identifying* as something is not enough to *make* you that something; a subjective feeling does not change physical realities in and of the world, and does not change the lived and felt experience of embodied experiences.

Chapter 2

'Gender Identity'

The introduction of the concept of 'gender identity' dates back to the 1950s. Psychologist John Money who founded the Gender Identity Clinic within Johns Hopkins University in the USA, is considered the 'father' of gender ideology. According to Money, "sexual identity is substantively a product of society and, therefore, ductile and malleable at birth."[8] In order to prove this theory, he carried out horrific experiments of surgical butchery, attempting 'gender reassignment' on girls and boys whose sexual traits at birth were considered 'ambiguous'. His best-known case is that of Bruce Reimer, a boy who had suffered penile damage during surgery shortly after birth. This researcher's Mengele-like morbid interest also stemmed from the fact that this child had a homozygous (i.e. genetically identical) twin, which made for a perfect case of observing their growth. Given the two brothers shared the same genetic heritage, the same family environment, and were both born of the same sex, Money could compare the psychosexual development of Brian, who was born and remained male, with that of Bruce who underwent surgery to

---

8 Enrica Perucchietti and Gianluca Marletta. *Unisex*. Bologna: Arianna Editrice. 2015, p. 46.

'become' female. Moreover, this was the first case in the history of medicine of a 'gender reassignment' conducted not on an intersex subject or one carrying congenital malformations or with sexual characteristics considered 'substandard', but on a subject born with intact male sex organs, which were mistakenly damaged at birth.

At the age of 22 months, in 1965, Bruce was operated on by Money's team: his testicles were amputated and a 'rudimentary external vagina' was remodelled. Bruce *became* Brenda and his parents raised him as a girl and allowed doctors to subject him to hormone treatment with oestrogen. Money explained to the family that the important thing was that they dressed him like a girl, did not cut his hair, and made him feel like a she and not a he. At the age of 13, Brenda threatened to commit suicide if forced to continue to attend Money's sessions. His parents then told him the truth of his story, and later he said: "For the first time everything made sense, and I understood who and what I was." He then underwent a long course of surgical (double mastectomy and two phalloplasty surgeries) and hormonal (testosterone injections) treatments to regain his masculine appearance and once again became Bruce. But by then his life was irrevocably altered and after his twin brother Brian's suicide on 5 May 2004, he also decided to take his own life with a shotgun blast.[9]

'Gender identity' is now said to be 'each person's internal and individual experience of gender', also so defined within Canadian

---

9   John Colapinto. *As Nature Made Him: The Boy Who Was Raised as a Girl.* New York and London: Harper Perennial. 2006.

legislation, but this definition misunderstands what gender is. The confusion between sex and gender, where gender means woman and man instead of the social construction of feminine and masculine, leads to further confusion. Gender is not about internal or individual experiences, it is a *social construction* as a means of consolidating precisely those stereotypes that, paradoxically, are instead reinforced by the very concept of 'gender identity':

> In the new wave of transgenderism, gender becomes biology. Instead of recognizing that gender is a social and political construct, trans advocates claim it is a personal issue of self-identification by declaration, with or without hormonal treatment and/or surgical intervention—a biological toggle switch to turn on and off at will.[10]

What is called 'gender identity' is actually an individual's perception of how his or her sex-linked and environmentally influenced personality compares with people of the same and opposite sex. In other words, it is a self-assessment of one's stereotypical degree of *masculinity* or *femininity* and is mistakenly confused with biological sex. This confusion stems from a cultural inability to understand the wide distribution of personalities and preferences within the sexes and a possible overlap between them.

When a girl reports that she 'feels like a boy' or 'is a boy' that sentiment may reflect her perception of how her personality and preferences compare with the rest of her peers. The lack of understanding of the existence of the different possible personalities

---

10 Janice G. Raymond. *Doublethink: A Feminist Challenge to Transgenderism*. Mission Beach: Spinifex Press. 2021, p. 3.

and behavioural differences related to sex has led to a confusion that has a strong impact especially on those boys and girls who would be more likely to become gay, lesbian or bisexual adults if they were allowed to fully experience their puberty without it being artificially suppressed:[11]

> Such ideas [sex-specific stereotypes concerning men and women] have been refuted, largely thanks to the feminist movement, but today, by creating and supporting the idea that a person might have 'an internal gender identity', we are going backwards. No one is born with a 'gender'. We are born male or female. Gender is imposed on us through our socialization.[12]

The Declaration on Women's Sex-Based Rights highlights what the real consequences of the concept of 'gender identity' are:

> The concept of 'gender identity' has enabled men who claim a female 'gender identity' to assert, in law, policies, and practice, that they are members of the category of women, which is a category based upon sex […] to be included in the category of lesbian, which is a category based upon sex […] [they] seek to be included in the legal category of mother […] [they] are being enabled to access opportunities and protections set aside for women.[13]

---

11 See William J. Malone. 'No Child is Born in the Wrong Body … and other thoughts on the concept of gender identity'. 2019. <https://4thwavenow.com/2019/08/19/no-child-is-born-in-the-wrong-body-and-other-thoughts-on-the-concept-of-gender-identity/>.

12 Meghan Murphy. 'Transgenrisme, effacement politique du sexe et capitalisme'. *Collectif anti-genre*. 2021.

13 *Declaration on Women's Sex-Based Rights*. <https://www.womensdeclaration.com/en/declaration-womens-sex-based-rights-full-text/>, accessed 10 September 2022.

With the introduction of the concept of 'gender identity' and 'gender self-ID', spaces reserved for women will have to open up to any man who says he identifies as a woman, or they risk having to close and no longer receive public funding, as happened in England for anti-violence centres and battered women's shelters.

It is also striking that trans claims represent only MtFs (short for alleged transition from male to female) who demand access to the rights of another group: women. They do not claim spaces of their own, but those of women; they do not claim words of their own, but those that belong to women:

> 'Gender identity' ideology allows for the opening of markets in identities [...] as it violates the physical boundary between males and females. So far, this violation is cosmetic only, a façade only made possible with modern technology, drugs, and surgeries. With advances in medical technology—especially regarding genetic manipulations such as CRISPR—and the normalization of this breach, potentially more significant encroachments to human sex, and humanity itself, loom large.[14]

In the medical field, the latest 'trans' trends affirm that 'gender identity' is said to be 'innate' from the time we are in our mother's womb, and that it derives from hormonal and genetic factors.[15]

---

14 Jennifer Bilek. 'Capturing the American Psychological Association: The Engineering of Human Sexual Evolution'. *The 11th Hour Blog.* <https://www.the11thhourblog.com/post/capturing-the-american-psychological-association-the-engineering-of-human-sexual-evolution>, accessed 25 October 2021.

15 Two articles as an example among the many published: <https://www.sciencedirect.com/science/article/abs/pii/B9780128159682000098?via%3Dihub>, accessed 20 April 2023; Jiska Ristori *et al.* 'Brain Sex Differences Related

Attributing a biological genesis to 'gender identity' is a short circuit of thought: gender identity, which among other things is based on social stereotypes, becomes a supposedly *innate* biological fact and acquires more importance than biological sex.

---

to Gender Identity Development: Genes or Hormones?' <https://pubmed.ncbi.nlm.nih.gov/32204531/>, accessed 20 April 2023.

Chapter 3

Women's Prisons in California and Canada

In California, after the implementation of the 'gender self-ID' law, men who say they identify as women can apply for transfer to women's prisons without even beginning hormone treatment as was required in the past. Currently, nearly 300 inmates simply declaring themselves as women have applied to be transferred to women's prisons for the less restrictive measures in force there. These inmates include those convicted of paedophilia, sex crimes and crimes against minors. The problematic nature of this situation is obvious. There have been many protests from female inmates alleging violence by male inmates, which has resulted in even more repressive and stringent measures in the organisation of prison life, to the detriment of women prisoners, to manage the presence of men. Just think of the shared spaces and time allocated for recreation in prison yards, for socialising, or even seemingly mundane daily tasks such as showering; spaces and moments that in a confined situation can become even more cramped.

In California's largest women's prison, shortly after the first men were transferred, condoms and the morning-after pill were distributed and 'new resources for pregnancy' were introduced, with posters hung in the infirmary outlining the options, including prenatal care, abortion and adoption:[16] a tacit admission of how sex and rape are predicted by the institution itself when women and men are forcibly made to live together inside a prison.[17]

A coalition of feminist organisations including WoLF (Women's Liberation Front), WHRC USA (Women's Human Rights Coalition, now Women's Declaration International), Save Women's Sports, and WLRN (Women's Liberation Radio News) have begun organising protests outside women's prisons,[18] allowing the many unheard voices of women prisoners to be heard.

In Canada, too, since the 'gender self-ID' law was passed, men who identify as women have been allowed to transfer to women's prisons.

Among many first-hand accounts, Kathy, a former prisoner, told of the sexual harassment she suffered in prison at the hands of a paedophile. Correctional Services of Canada had dismissed her complaints by labelling them as bigotry and threatening to put her in isolation.

---

16 Complete text of the poster provided by a source in prison: <https://static1.squarespace.com/static/5f232ea74d8342386a7ebc52/t/60f08279f347573036abbbe9/1626374777209/>; Screenshot_20210715-013753_JPay+%28copy%29.jpg.
17 'Californias B 132: a disaster for women'. <https://www.womensliberationfront.org/california-sb-132-a-disaster-for-incarcerated-women>, accessed 7 October 2021.
18 <https://www.womensliberationfront.org/news/feminists-protest-men-housed-in-washington-womens-prisons>, accessed 7 October 2021.

A movement of resistance arose around Heather Mason, a former prisoner and activist, who wrote an open letter to the Executive Director of the Canadian Association of Elizabeth Fry Societies (CAEFS) dealing with the plight of imprisoned women with children. The following words by Heather Mason are significant:

> We think back to the situation for women in the 1930s when a tunnel was built between P4W (Prison for Women) and Kingston Penitentiary so that women could be carried underground, to be sexually abused by male prisoners. What has changed? The tunnel is now ideological, and all it takes is a transfer.[19]

In the UK, the High Court in 2021 ruled that a Ministry of Justice policy, which allowed prisoners to be housed according to their 'gender identity', "irrespective of whether they have taken any legal or medical steps to acquire that gender," was lawful.[20]

---

19 Barbara Kay. 'The complicated truth about transwomen in women's prisons'. <https://nationalpost.com/opinion/barbara-kay-the-complicated-truth-about-transwomen-in-womens-prisons>, accessed 7 July 2021.

20 Marina Terragni. 'UK come Canada e California. Corpi maschili nelle carceri femminili'. In *Feminist Post*. <https://feministpost.it/dal-mondo/uk-come-canada-e-california-corpi-maschili-nelle-carceri-femminili-lo-ribadisce-la-camera-dei-lord/>, accessed 7 July 2021.

Chapter 4

Gender 'Neutral' Ideology in Schools

A look at other countries, especially the most 'up-to-date' ones, is useful to understand the direction taken and the actual consequences of ideologies full of catchy rhetoric that are entrenched behind the words of 'freedom' and 'equality', now emptied of their meaning.

In Canada, indoctrination into 'gender identity' has become the norm in schools and, as a result, boys and girls as young as 11 are demanding that their *preferred pronouns* be used and many teenagers are calling themselves *pansexuals*. In May 2021, research teams from two Canadian universities proposed The Gegi Project—a unicorn—which aims to teach boys and girls from kindergarten to seventh grade that sex does not exist and to give them the tools "normally possessed only by legal professionals" to change their school's regulations in the name of "affirming their gender identity." Gegi is the unicorn representing 'gender identity' and is supposed to help boys and girls "advocate for your gender expression and gender identity human rights at school."[21]

---

21 <https://www.gegi.ca/>.

Gegi stands for Gender Expression Gender Identity and at the same time, it happens to be synonymous with vulva in urban slang, in a distinctly insulting and negative sense. *Urbandictionary* now suggests it as a "nice nickname" for someone named Georgi, but a year ago, the definition—clearly removed on pressure from Canada—was far less *nice*.[22] Strange coincidence.

In Canada, boys and girls of all ages are now taught that they have a 'gender identity', which is more significant than biological sex. School policy allows for 'social transition' without parents being informed. One father learned that his daughter was referred to by a male name only when he read it in the seventh grade yearbook. It turns out to be significant, and a dangerous and troubling precedent, that this father, who opposed the administration of puberty blockers to his daughter, was sentenced to six months in jail and a $30,000 fine.[23]

"These children are not your children," cried an American mother, breaking the silence and censorship by denouncing the trans and queer indoctrination to which little girls and boys, ages five to 13, in American and Canadian elementary and middle schools, are subjected. Among the latest books of trans propaganda read in classrooms is *Felix Ever After* in which the main character is 'a trans person'. The cover image shows prominent surgical scars on her chest: a little girl with an irreversible

---

22 <https://web.archive.org/web/20210422105059/https://www.urbandictionary.com/define.php?term=gegi>.
23 Bruce Bower. "'A Certain Madness Amok": In Canada, trans "justice" has gone haywire'. <https://www.city-journal.org/canadian-father-jailed-for-speaking-out-about-trans-identifying-child>, accessed 22 November 2021.

mastectomy. The mother thus concluded her speech, "You ought to be ashamed. Never forget that silence is tacit approval."[24]

And for the youngest children, there is no shortage of cartoons and songs with 'trans' characters to inculcate from an early age that there can be two 'mothers' (one of which might be a biological man), two fathers (one of whom might be a biological woman) and that sex is not binary.[25]

In Australia, *The Gender Fairy*, a 2015 book by Jo Hirst, was aimed at "transgender girls and boys" and their families and is read in primary school. The book is intended as an "educational resource for children ages four and up" and is designed to be read aloud at home or in the classroom. The book aims to reassure boys and girls by saying "only you know if you are a boy or a girl. No one can tell you."[26]

The Gender Fairy is just one of the many picture books for girls and boys now in vogue in western countries including in US schools and alternative families; books that create dangerous confusion for those boys and girls struggling with their development. They instil an even more dangerous notion that you can

---

24 YouTube. 'Mom speaking out at Puyallup School Board Meeting against the exploitation and sexualization of kids'. <https://www.youtube.com/watch?v=l3OwGnXuWP4>; and 'Questi bambini non sono vostri: la rivolta di una madre americana contro la trans-propaganda nelle scuole'. <https://feministpost.it/magazine/primo-piano/questi-bambini-non-sono-vostri-la-rivolta-di-una-madre-americana-contro-la-trans-propaganda-nelle-scuole/>, accessed 10 September 2022.

25 You Tube. 'The Blue's Clues Pride Parade'. <https://www.youtube.com/watch?v=d4vHegf3WPU>, accessed November 2021.

26 Jo Hirst. *The Gender Fairy*. Victoria: Oban Road Publishing. 2015.

be whatever you want to be, as if acting a role in a play. But real life is not a performance—despite what Butler & Co claim—and while in a play we can put on and take off a mask, in real life we internalise the idea that we can transform our body by losing all sense of boundaries.

These new books for girls and boys are part of a progressive rewriting and transformation of the classics—books, films, cartoons—in the language of political correctness. The classic story *Snow White and the Seven Dwarfs* is under indictment in the court of political correctness as the prince's kiss was given without consent because Snow White was asleep!

In France, in the new children's book version of *The Five Jugglers' Club,* the little girl who used to cry now no longer cries; she used to cook and now she no longer cooks; the street vendors who distrusted the police now no longer distrust them; the uncle who used to organise a robbery now does nothing like that; the fact that the child was raised for money disappears, as does everything that might refer to a difficult and complex life. Of course, in the new version the boys and girls have mobile phones.

Fewer words, less difficult words, fewer and poorer sentences and phrases, less but more ideologically oriented sense and meaning, less narrative variety, and poorer and poorer narratives about the world. Everything is sweetened and glittered. There is no need to burn books, just rewrite them. It is an attack on the capacity to develop critical thinking and thus on the very possibility of developing critical awareness; an attack that begins to mould girls and boys from an early age, building empty, superficial, depthless, sterile, neutral, fluid individuals, for a voluntary servitude necessary for the transhuman and posthuman project.

Chapter 5

In Europe: The Matić Report

On 23 June 2021, the Matić Report was voted on and adopted at the plenary of the European Parliament, regarding the state of sexual and reproductive health and related rights in the EU, in the context of women's health.

It says *women's health*, but the words 'women' and 'sex' have been replaced with gender.[27]

Although not legally binding, adoption of the Matić Report resolutions means that UN member states have been called on to follow precise guidelines that have been outlined. This Report includes the concept of 'gender identity'. It

> calls on member states [...] to reform laws, policies and practices that exclude certain groups from access to maternity, pregnancy and birth-related care, including by removing discriminatory legal and policy restrictions that apply on grounds of sexual orientation or gender identity.

---

27 'UN Adopts Resolutions to Protect Gender and Reproductive Rights'. <https://reproductiverights.org/un-general-assembly-resolutions-gender-reproductive-rights/>.

It includes the concept of 'reproductive rights', setting out to overcome obstacles that cause limited "access to fertility treatments" by extending medically assisted reproduction. It

> calls on the Member States to ensure that all persons of reproductive age have access to fertility treatments, regardless [...] of their gender identity or sexual orientation; [...] calls on the Member States to take a holistic, rights-based, inclusive and non-discriminatory approach to fertility, including measures to prevent infertility, and ensuring equality of access to services for all persons of reproductive age, and to make medically assisted reproduction available and accessible in Europe.[28]

In the directions it says that

> transgender men and non-binary persons may also undergo pregnancy and should, in such cases, benefit from measures for pregnancy and birth-related care without discrimination on the basis of their gender identity.

The direction at the European level as well as internationally is clear: accept 'gender identity', gender-neutral ideology, artificial reproduction.

Compulsory LGBTQ+ teaching is arriving in English schools: coloring manuals with 'trans' characters for five-year-old girls and boys, manuals that teach nine-year-old girls and boys how to masturbate, manuals for twelve-year-olds that teach that sex does not exist. In addition to instilling the idea that one may have been

---

28 <https://www.europarl.europa.eu/doceo/document/A-9-2021-0169_EN.html>.

born in 'the wrong body', the promotion of early sexualisation in the name of 'inclusion' is making headway, which will also serve to clear paedophilia as a new 'sexual orientation'.[29]

---

29   Chris Matthews. 'Twelve-year-olds are being taught about anal sex in school while nine-year-olds are told to 'masturbate' for homework: The shocking lesson plans used by teachers in UK classrooms'. In *Mail Online*, 18 June 2023, <https://www.dailymail.co.uk/news/article-12189041/Twelve-year-olds-taught-anal-sex-school-nine-year-olds-told-masturbate.html>, accessed 27 June 2023.

Chapter 6

France and Spain: Significant New Legislative Steps

In multiple countries we see legislative proposals that include 'gender identity', 'self-ID', and expanding access to medically assisted procreation (MAP) techniques.

France, with its new bioethics law that also provides access to MAP techniques for all women,[30] is leading the way for LGBTQ+ movement demands in other countries.

The new French bioethics law that came into effect in early July 2021 is an important step: it allows any woman—partnered with a man, partnered with a woman, or alone—to have access to MAP techniques. For couples consisting of two women, motherhood is conferred upon both of them. In other words, being a mother is established through a simple declaration of will,

---

30 For further information, see Silvia Guerini, 'Considerazioni intorno alla nuova legge francese di bioetica. È aperta la strada alla riproduzione artificiale dell'umano. Contro l'eugenetica e l'antropocidio riaffermiamo con forza l'indisponibilità dei corpi e del vivente'. <https://www.resistenzealnanomondo.org/necrotecnologie/biotecnologie/considerazioni-intorno-alla-nuova-legge-francese-di-bioetica-e-aperta-la-strada-alla-riproduzione-artificiale-dellumano-contro-leugenetica-e-lantropocidio-riaffermiamo-con-forza-lindisponib-2/>, accessed 14 February 2022.

so that, by law, the distinction between the woman giving birth and the other woman is dropped. Moreover, the establishment of filiation no longer provides for the indication of paternal lineage. It will allow conception of an embryo to occur using both gametes, male and female, to be derived from donation, opening up a biomarket of gametes. It will allow for the cryopreservation of oocytes without medical grounds and in vitro fertilization (IVF) with three parents (sperm, eggs and mitochondrial DNA from another woman).

With a *declaration of will, declaration of intent, mother of intention, parents of intention, parental project*, the human being ceases to have a history or origins. The human being is reduced to the eugenic assembly of egg and sperm for a narcissistic and selfish desire for a child at all costs by a consumer, who in some countries can already order a manufactured embryo according to his or her own tastes by *programming* it through the selection of certain characteristics, including sex.

Being or not being a biological mother, which characterises motherhood as a condition intrinsically linked to a woman's body, is stripped of any meaning in the new French law. In this profoundly eugenic vision, the human subject, through technology, can and must free him- or herself from the bodily conditions of their existence in order to realise their individual desires.

The rhetoric of *equality*, in which the extension of the possibility of using MAP techniques for lesbian couples and single women has been clothed, masks the real meaning of this law:

the new law opens the right to these techniques, including IVF with intracytoplasmic sperm injection (ICSI), to *all* women by opening up the artificial reproduction of human beings through a process that begins with a plastic insemination tube and ends with the genetic selection of embryos.

The law moves toward a gradual extension of pre-implantation genetic diagnosis (PGD), a eugenic extension in line with the openings of national laws in various European countries in which there has been a shift from the prohibition of PGD to the possibility of using it in the first instance to avoid the transmission of serious genetic diseases, later to avoid the transmission of probable-onset diseases up to less serious conditions bordering on blemishes such as crossed eyes.[31]

The same law, in the area of research, will allow experimentation on human embryos without the need for exceptions, and the time of embryo development allowed to be experimented on will be extended to 21 days. This law will further increase human embryonic stem cell research, allow the creation of artificial gametes, chimeric human-animal embryos that can be implanted in other animals, and genetically modified human embryos for research purposes, thus paving the way for genetically modified children.

The new French law on bioethics is a profoundly eugenic law: it permits the crossing of the species barrier, it allows a

---

31 In 2007, the British authority for MAP authorised recourse to PGD to avoid the birth of a cross-eyed child.

selection of embryos to be implanted to 'use' them as 'medicine' for an older sibling, and sanctions embryo modification using the CRISPR/Cas9 technique, transforming the human being into an organism to be genetically modified. On paper, this law still prohibits the implantation and gestation of genetically modified embryos; however, it allows the first steps toward children being genetically tailored to the wishes of parent-clients.

The Left screams 'MAP for all and everyone' and hurls the accusation of 'discrimination' against anyone who criticises the concept of 'womb for rent' (surrogacy) and MAP, branding them homophobic and reactionary. The dissident voices of radical feminists and lesbians in France are similarly accused of 'discrimination'. These include Marie-Jo Bonnet, a feminist and militant lesbian, founder of the Women's Liberation Movement (MLF), and among the first lesbian feminists critical of so-called 'gestation for others' (GPA, surrogacy) and medically assisted procreation:

> But reproductive freedom cannot come through lab rooms, and *MAP for all* is not a cry for emancipation, but a future to which we may all be condemned:
>
> This cyborg-liberal left misrepresents the struggle for individual freedom with an apologia for mercantile freedom. It confuses political equality with biological uniformity of individuals. It dreams of a liberal eugenics, the abolition of the body and the [introduction of the] artificial womb. It fantasizes a posthumanity through the technological re-creation of the human species. Under

the guise of transgression and rebellion [it promises] enthusiastic adherence to technocapitalism.[32]

In France, in January 2022, a new law was passed against conversion therapies,[33] practices that were already criminally punishable. In a society that in the past year has seen deconstruction go so far as to depict a Santa Claus in a pink tutu and Mary Magdalene with a beard, the danger was certainly not the possibility of a return to the terrible conversion therapies for homosexuals and lesbians, but if anything, the imposition of the new 'fluid', transgender and transhuman normality by *not* allowing talking therapies: called the new conversion therapies.

Indeed, it is no coincidence that 'gender identity' is included in this law in order to "prohibit practices aimed at altering a person's sexual orientation or gender identity."[34] This too is part of the process that erases family ties—this law, in fact, provides for the partial or total revocation of parental responsibility for parents who oppose the transition path for their young children.

Significant in this direction is a 2019 document[35] produced by the multinational giant law firm Dentons in collaboration with the Thomson Reuters Foundation and the International Lesbian, Gay, Bisexual, Transgender, Queer & Intersex Youth

---

32 Alexis Escudero. *La riproduzione artificiale dell'umano*. Aprilia: Ortica Editrice. 2016, p. 3.

33 Various psychiatric practices, including electroshock, aimed to change the sexual orientation of a person from homosexual to heterosexual.

34 <https://www.assemblee-nationale.fr/dyn/15/textes/l15b4021_proposition-loi>.

35 <https://www.iglyo.com/wp-content/uploads/2019/11/IGLYO_v3-1.pdf>.

and Student Organization (IGLYO)—the original name for IGLYO originally stood for International Gay and Lesbian Youth Organisation—that outlines government policies that can be drawn upon in order to limit the ability of parents to obstruct the transition path of their children so that 'gender transitions' can take place even without their consent:

> The IGLYO *et al.* (2019) report has many flaws including ignoring the need to discuss the long-term health consequences for teenagers wanting to transition. The report asks for the elimination of the minimum age requirement as well as being in favour of self-determined change of identity as quickly as possible. None of this takes account of the possibility of infertility, cancer, bone density loss and other as yet unforeseen health impacts. But these big media companies (Reuters), large law firms (Dentons) and organisations that used to have the words lesbian and gay in their names and their mission statements now pander almost solely to the 'needs' of the transgender lobby."[36]

In Spain, the 'Ley Trans' law, pushed through by the transactivist organisation, reopens access to lesbian or single women to MAP techniques provided by the national health service (a possibility that had been eliminated seven years ago), including, for the first time, for "trans people with gestational capacity."[37] Similar

---

36 Susan Hawthorne. *Vortex: The Crisis of Patriarchy.* Mission Beach: Spinifex Press. 2020, p. 208.
37 'Sanidad financiará la reproducción asistida a las "personas trans con capacidad gestante."' *El Pais.* 2021. <https://elpais.com/sociedad/2021-11-05/sanidad-financiara-la-reproduccion-asistida-a-las-personas-trans-con-capacidad-gestante.html>.

to France, in a female couple, both will figure as mothers and there will no longer be a distinction between the woman who gave birth and the other woman. In the text of the law, the term 'mother' is replaced with that of 'gestating spouse': the path of resignification and evaporation of the mother and ultimately also of the woman. The boundaries of the concept mother are diluted to the point of making 'mother' indefinable and therefore completely meaningless: if everyone and anyone can be a mother, no one is a mother any more, forgetting that once upon a time *mater semper certa est.*

Today we have a mother who rents her womb, a genetic mother who sells her eggs and becomes the mother who provides DNA, and a commissioning mother, in the new assisted reproduction technology ROPA (Partner's Oocyte Reception, also called "double maternity"). For female couples we have a genetic mother and a pregnant mother.

We have parent one and parent two, not father and mother, which fits perfectly into the postmodern queer framework of erasing the material reality of bodies. Now it is about establishing an individual who is nothing more than an indistinct, variable, infinitely malleable and manipulable object of consumption.

Ley Trans has worked to expand the ability of children to 'self-ID' their 'gender' without parental oversight. For children aged 12 to 14, a judge can decide whether the child possesses sufficient maturity to self-ID his or her gender. Before the age of 12 it would still be possible for a child to change name. Some parental consent would be required for a child under the age of

16 to transition, but in minors between the ages of 14 and 16, if the parents deny consent, the minor is placed in the care of a guardian. In effect, this denies the parents' ability to oppose transitioning: the children—boys and girls—are wrested from parental authority by a techno-medical system that forcefully enters the lives of these children by assessing their problems and difficulties and deciding on whether or not to begin the transition.

In Spain the radical feminist movement has taken to the streets against Ley Trans.[38] From one of their communiqués we read: "[...] repeal of the Trans Laws." Yes, in plural, 'Trans Laws', because they include all legislation that replaces the legal category of 'sex' with 'gender identity'.

Added to this are the so-called Trans Laws, LGTBI Laws and Zerolo Laws, which were approved in the Spanish Parliament on 16 February 2023. These laws criminalise people who, in the exercise of their fundamental right to freedom of expression, defend the use of the words 'woman', 'mother', 'vulva', or 'err' in the use of pronouns:

> We also call for the repeal of transnational regional legislation including, among others, 15 laws on 'gender self-determination', 14 educational protocols and 15 health-care protocols that allow—even in the absence of a national law recognising the right to self-determination—sex determination, the implementation

---

38 'A favor de la agenda feminista y contra las leyes trans'. June 2021. <https://feministes.cat/blog/agenda-feminista-contra-lleis-trans>, accessed 27 April 2023.

of sexist educational policies, the violation of women's sex-based rights (allowing men access to our spaces and perverting statistics), and the indiscriminate hormone treatment of children. [...] Finally, we denounce the use of transnational legislation to allow rapists and murderers access to women's prisons; we are outraged and indignant about this.[39]

Today we cannot fail to recall the murder of Vanesa Santana in Fuerteventura, whose rapist and murderer, Jonathan Robaina, declared himself a woman on the first day of his trial (just three days after the unanimous approval of the Ley Trans in the Parliament of the Canary Islands). Luckily, a team of forensic experts was able to make a convincing intervention. Otherwise, a man would have been able to be transferred to a women's prison because Ley Trans had been passed in the Canary Islands three days before this court case.

The case of Catalonia is emblematic of the current trend in all countries. Since the creation, in 2012, of the Servei Trànsit, specialising in 'gender dysphoria', the number of people undertaking the 'transition' path has quadrupled and more than half are women. Between 2012 and 2021, one third were minors and two thirds were under 25. The average age has dropped from 35 in 2012 to around 23 today. Up to the age of nine, most are boys,

---

39 'Feminist Manifesto'. 26 June 2021. Translated into Italian at <https://feministpost.it/dal-mondo/la-spagna-riapre-alla-ley-trans-improvviso-voltafaccia-del-psoe/>, accessed 29 April 2023. Original in Spanish at <chrome-extension://efaidnbmnnnibpcajpcglclefindmkaj/https://feministes.cat/wp-content/uploads/manifiesto-26J-2>.

from ten to 25 most are girls; above 30, men predominate. Most cases of minors are girls; most cases of adults are men.[40]

Faced with this situation, we cannot help but ask ourselves: why do girls no longer want to become women? Why are girls and boys increasingly confused about their sex?

The techno-medical system with all the harmful consequences of its operation has no interest in questioning itself in this regard. Artificial Intelligence with its calculability acts towards those consequences that represent the protocols of whoever programmed it, such as towards a repetitive assembly line, but in this case it is a disassembly in a fluid universe.

The 'Self-ID law' is also arriving in Germany. The proposed law would provide 'gender self-ID certification' also for minors. Parental consent would be required for children under the age of 14. From the age of 14, if the parents deny consent, the child is entrusted to the Family Court. After a year, the gender change can be cancelled, after another year changed again … and so on, every year you can 'choose' whether to be a woman or a man and then who knows what else …[41]

A multiplication of synthetic identities for bodies redesigned in the laboratory, for selected and engineered embryos, for gene therapies, for "new GMOs—TEAs". They prepare us for endless disassembly and reassembly, they prepare us for a GMO life.

---

40 'Informe Trànsit: De hombres adultos a niñas adolescentes'. <https://feministes.cat/es/publicaciones/informe-transit-cataluna-2022>, accessed 29 April 2023.

41 By the time of going to press in July 2023, the Self-ID laws in Germany remain a proposal, strongly opposed by radical feminists and a few parliamentarians including right-wing members.

Chapter 7

Steps Forward in Italy

In Italy, the Zan Bill (DDL Zan) envisaged a

> therapeutic project with the signing of a treatment agreement between specialists, parents and the child who between the ages of 5 and 8 will be able to choose his or her gender identity.[42]

It is only a matter of time for similar proposals to take root. During a demonstration in Milan in support of the Zan Bill, a representative of Famiglie Arcobaleno (Rainbow Families) and Sinistra Italiana (Italian Left) put it clearly:

> … the real goals are self-ID of gender and the right to surrogacy […] The Zan Bill is a law with a long-term outlook; it looks to the future. The next step is changing Law 40 [Law 40/2004 grants MAP only to infertile couples], which leaves behind single women who cannot access ART. We want the revision of the now old law 164/82 on transitional pathways [i.e., obtaining free 'gender self-ID']. We want a season of rights where we talk about MAP and surrogacy,

---

42 DDL means 'Disegno di Legge' and is the initial phase of law making in Italy. DDL Zan refers to the law proposed by Alessandro Zan whose main demands are outlined in this section. A 'season of rights' is an Italian expression.

and recognition of the sons and daughters of rainbow families. The Zan Bill is just the beginning.[43]

Also at the 2021 Milan Pride March, a representative of Rainbow Families called for birth certificates to record the details of the non-biological parent and for "free access to assisted reproduction techniques for one and all."[44]

On 27 October 2021, the approval process of the Zan Bill was blocked in the Senate. But there is no cause for celebration as we are well aware that the proposed legislation against 'homolesbotransphobia' will actually serve to mask the introduction of the concept of 'gender identity' and 'gender self-ID' and will be a pretext for censoring any dissident position and any criticism of the gender 'neutral' trans agenda.

Claiming that surrogacy is bodily exploitation will be prosecuted as a hate crime, under the guise that such a claim is discrimination against homosexual parents. Asserting that we are women *and not menstruating people* or *lesbians with penises* or that we have a vagina *and not a front hole* will be prosecutable as deemed discriminatory against 'transgender' people.

Replacing, in these new bills, 'gender identity' with 'transgender identity', as proposed by some 'feminists' and associations

---

43 Video of the speech can be found at <https://www.facebook.com/watch/?v=1954485998061160>.
44 'Autocertificazione di genere, utero in affitto: il Ddl Zan serve a questo'. In Feminist Post. <https://feministpost.it/italy/libera-autocertificazione-di-genere-utero-in-affitto-il-ddl-zan-serve-a-questo-detto-con-chiarezza-dal-palco-di-milano/>, accessed 29 April 2023.

belonging to the (LGB)TQ+ movement, does not actually unhinge the framework and confirms the 'gender identity' industry in which being a woman, far from being a bodily condition, becomes a subjective feeling and something that can be bought in the new biomarket of desires, thus reaffirming violence against women's bodies that reduces them to artifacts.[45]

Elly Schlein, the current secretary of the Democratic Party (PD), voted against an amendment condemning surrogacy when she was a MEP (Member of the European Parliament) in December 2018. It is enough to read her program on page 14: "More courage on LGBTQIA+ rights": "a law against homolesbotransphobia," "full recognition of the rights of same-parent families," "make transition paths simpler and more accessible by overcoming law 164 of 1982 and introducing alias careers," "may our schools open the doors to effective and sexual education of the new generations," "an Italy in which affirming one's gender identity is no longer the result of an obstacle course, but the elementary recognition of a human right."

In a nutshell: This is the agenda of 'trans'feminism and transhumanism. It is no coincidence that in the document 'Reliable allies in the European Parliament'[46] released by George Soros' Open Society to indicate friendly MEPs, we find Elly Schlein

---

[45] Janice G. Raymond. *The Transsexual Empire: The Making of the She-Male*. Boston: Beacon Press. 1979.

[46] 'Reliable allies in the European Parliament (2014—2019)'. <chrome-extension:// efaidnbmnnnibpcajpcglclefindmkaj/https://legacy.gscdn.nl/archives/images/ soroskooptbrussel.pdf>.

listed for her commitment to LGBTQ+ causes. Schlein has appointed Alessandro Zan as rights manager for the Democratic Party. In other words, the links are clear.

In Italy, since March 2018, following a favourable opinion from the Bioethics Commission, the administration of a triptorelin-based drug for the purpose of blocking hormonal activity to minors has been authorised. Its use was granted off-label, that is, outside the prescription guidelines of the drug itself and placed under the responsibility of individual prescribing doctors. It was also included within the category of treatments provided in basic levels of public health care.

It is impossible to know how many minors are treated, as very little information leaks out. But the transition paths for children and adolescents are growing worryingly and seriously in Italy too. The Careggi University Hospital in Florence, one of the main specialised centres in the field of 'diagnosis and therapy of gender incongruity' and for treatments in adolescents, took charge of 40 adolescents during 2020.

Since the drug was authorised off-label in 2018, in the city of Turin alone—in the Molinette and Regina Margherita hospitals—diagnoses of 'gender dysphoria' among minors have increased from one to 37 until 2022. The hospital that carries out the most operations is that of Pisa, which went from six in 2011, when it started, to 60 in 2021. Instead at San Camillo in Rome in the first three months of 2021, the number of minors with 'dysphoria of gender' grew by 150% compared to the same period of the previous year. In 2021 at the University Hospital of Palermo, requests for interventions have grown by 30%.[47]

The guidelines adopted in Italy refer to the 'gender affirmative model' and provide for an evaluation of at least six months, which in fact translates into one session per month, for a total of six sessions before any medical interventions are undertaken. The reports collected by parents from these medical centres all agree that the path does not have the intention of exploring and understanding the discomfort of young people and bringing its causes to light, but rather of directing him or her along the path of 'transition'.

The University Hospital of Padua is preparing to become an important new centre for 'gender identity', a centre which will also provide the option of cryopreserving ova and sperm cells in the public health system for people who will undertake the 'transition' path, attempting to induce institutional systems to include cryopreservation itself in LEA (essential levels of assistance) charged to the national health system. This is contrary to what is happening today where the cryopreservation of gametes from those who start the transition path is expected to take place exclusively in the private health system. This is a change that can only mean that the number of 'transitions' will increase, with all that follows, such as the sterilisation of adolescents and young women and men.

---

47 Silvana Palazzo. 'Boom di giovani che cambiano sesso/Disforia di genere, al San Camillo +150% accessi'. In *Il Sussidiario*. 2021. <www.ilsussidiario.net/news/boom-di-giovani-che-cambiano-sesso-disforia-di-genere-al-san-camillo-150-accessi/2171672/>.

It is useful to look to the field of bioethics to understand the state of progress of bioethical debates for certain techno-scientific developments. This offers us a broader framework in which to frame individual steps. It is significant that in the recent article 'Uterus Transplantation and the Redefinition of Core Bioethics Precepts' by two Rome University researchers, they open up the possibility of a man giving birth:

> ... it is not unreasonable to assume that in transgender women, UTx [uterus transplantation] may go a long way towards the achievement of reproductive aspirations, benefit quality of life overall, and be effective in allaying dysphoric symptoms. [...] if UTx becomes mainstream, safe and effective for biological women with AUFI [absolute infertility of the uterine factor], would there be any morally tenable grounds as to why transgender women [men] should be denied such an opportunity for gestation? [...] such an option will mark a point where the set of moral and ethical precepts which we espouse could soon become obsolete.

And they continue:

> Advances in embryo manipulation through genome editing could soon pave the way for the eradication of diseases before birth, or even the enhancement of humans yet to be born, a whole new frontier in beginning of life bioethics for which we are unprepared. Ultimately, we feel it may all go down to whether procreative liberty ought to be deemed as entailing an absolute right to gestate, and whether transgender women [men] can be denied such a right without infringing upon ethical precepts of equality and non-

discrimination. Current bioethics approaches need to undergo a radical update.[48]

The point of no return is near.

---

[48] Federica Umani Ronchi and Gabriele Napoletano. 'Uterus Transplantation and the redefinition of core bioethics precepts'. In *Acta Biomed*. 2021. <https://pubmed.ncbi.nlm.nih.gov/34738555/>.

Chapter 8

Where Are We in Italy?

Currently, in the first quarter of 2023, the vast majority of Italians has absolutely no idea about what 'gender ideology' means. In fact, many people are convinced that it doesn't exist; that it is nothing more than an invention from some undetermined groups of far-right Catholic fanatics. "Gender ideology doesn't exist"[49] is the current mantra that you will hear in Italian progressive left circles. But, paradoxically, the first to claim that gender ideology doesn't exist are precisely those who propagate it most fervently.[50] In the world of LGBT, queer and 'trans'feminist activism, in particular the classic tactic of 'bringing everything back to Hitler' is used to discredit all dissent, accusing anyone who opposes 'gender ideology' of transphobia, bigotry, intolerance and fascism.

Moreover, if we step outside the ideologised and politicised world of activism, very few people are aware of the danger caused by a system of thought that, by asserting the primacy of subjective self-perception ('gender identity') over objective

---

49 'Does gender ideology not exist?' *Il Mondo Nuovo* 2.0. <https://www.youtube.com/watch?v=DrEZzvlD-KM&t=1s>.
50 'Alessandro Zan claims to *La Repubblica* that "gender theory is a made-up thing."' 23 October 2020. <https://www.youtube.com/watch?v=g0DUXogAIF8>.

reality (biological sex), aims to redefine the collective perception of reality.

Very few people know that the definitions of 'man' and 'woman' have been changed, as have, consequently, the definitions of 'heterosexuality' and 'homosexuality'.[51] Very few are aware of the phenomenon of so-called child transitions, of detransitioners, or of social contagion among adolescents and young adults (especially among girls). Nor are they informed about the countless problems caused abroad by self-ID, from the intrusion of men into private spaces, prisons and women's sports, to the social and legal persecution of those who do not bend to the dogma of 'gender identity'.

Most Italians do not even know the difference between the concepts of sexual orientation and 'gender identity', confusing 'gay' with 'trans' as if they were the same thing. This is how Italian queer transactivism—just like Anglo-Saxon transactivism—achieves its successes: equating the image of the homosexual with the ill-defined image of the transgender, uniting LGB with TQ+. But it is clear by now, and witnessed by groups such as the LGB Alliance[52] and Gays Against Groomers,[53] that internationally, much of the homosexual world does *not* want to be associated with the medicalisation and indoctrination of minors, nor with the supremacy of 'gender identity' over biological sex, a supremacy

---

51 'To know more about the new definitions of "sex," "gender," "gender identity" and so on: Le incongruenze logiche dell'ideologia gender (Part 1)'. *Il Mondo Nuovo* 2.0. <https://www.youtube.com/watch?v=Ad4rCo_7pfE>.
52 LGB Alliance. <https://lgballiance.org.uk/>.
53 Gays Against Groomers. <https://www.gaysagainstgroomers.com/>.

that harms, in addition to women and children, homosexuals themselves, who are now considered bigots and transphobic if they refuse to include the opposite sex in their sexual and sentimental attraction.[54]

By forcibly linking homosexuality with transgenderism, queer activists (well-infiltrated in corporations, institutions, and the media) present gender issues by disguising it as a generic 'fight for gay rights' and 'fight against bullying and discrimination'.

---

54 To know more about the incompatibility between transgenderism and homosexuality: 'The "inclusive" approach of transactivism (Part 2) — Homosexuals'. *Il Mondo Nuovo* 2.0. <https://www.youtube.com/watch?v=V64udsrrHMw>.

Chapter 9

Unicorns and Inclusivity: How Gender Ideology Enters Italian Schools[55]

It is especially through the rhetoric of anti-bullying that gender ideology quietly creeps into Italian schools, especially through external projects in which LGBTQ+ activists expose children and youth to concepts such as those of 'gender identity', gender fluidity, 'non-binary', and 'sex assigned at birth'. And so, through graphic models such as the Gender Unicorn and the Genderbread Person, Italian students learn that human sexual dimorphism does not exist and that 'woman' and 'man' are nothing more than subjective inner feelings.[56]

No one, except for a few feminists and (unlistened to) groups associated with Catholic-leaning activism, opposes the introduction of these ideological concepts—passed off as 'scientific truths'—into our country's schools, and this happens

---

[55] To know more about gender propaganda abroad and in Italy: 'Child transitions (Part 2)—Gender propaganda' *Il Mondo Nuovo* 2.0. <https://www.youtube.com/watch?v=L-iJTekW9ns&t=1294s>.

[56] *Quarta Repubblica*. 'Transgender propaganda enters schools'. 20 February 2023. <https://mediasetinfinity.mediaset.it/video/quartarepubblica/la-propaganda-transgender-entra-nelle-scuole_F312336401007C20>.

because almost no one, neither among parents nor teachers, is aware of what is really being taught in schools.

Often, it is the teachers themselves, instructed through special training courses,[57] who preach gender ideology to their students. Most are simply convinced that they are educating children about respect and inclusion (after all, these are the key words), while some ideologically-driven teachers proudly follow guides such as Classe Arcobaleno,[58] which are Italian adaptations of manuals produced by US LGBTQ associations. In these guides, neutral language is used (an asterisk * and a schwa ǝ) and it is explained, against all principles of reality, that "everyone decides their gender identity independently" and that "any person can identify with whatever makes them feel good and therefore their 'gender identity' cannot be questioned."

All this should not surprise us, especially if we examine the UNESCO guidelines reported in the *International Technical Guidance on Sexuality Education*.[59] Suffice to say that in the

---

57 An example of these training courses is 'I, YOU, US. Valuing differences in school: pathways and tools' (training course for teachers of middle and high schools) sponsored by, among others, the EU and the Ministry of Labor and Social Policy. <https://www.adl-zavidovici.eu/2023/02/02/io-tu-noi-corso-di-formazione-rete-antidiscriminazioni-brescia/>.

58 *RAINBOW CLASSROOM (A guide to acting in support of lesbian, gay, bisexual, transgender, queer, intersex, and other identity students in your school)*—Italian adaptation of the Safe Space Kit manual produced by GLSEN, a US-based LGBTQ association dedicated to "creating LGBTQ-inclusive schools." <https://risorselgbti.eu/wp-content/uploads/2022/07/cr-classe_arcobaleno-manuale-A5-web.pdf>.

59 UNESCO. *International Technical Guidance on Sexuality Education: An evidence-informed approach*. 2018. <https://www.unfpa.org/sites/default/

2009 version, the expression 'gender identity' appeared twice and in 2018 44 times. In this UN guidance, where ideological definitions of sex, gender and 'gender identity' are provided, the learning objectives for ages five to eight are to "define the difference between sex and gender and reflect on how one feels about one's sex and gender." Thus, elementary school children are actively pushed to question their own sexed body and the nebulous 'gender identity': a concept that is described as 'innate' but is actually based on conformity to rigid sexist stereotypes of masculinity and femininity.

In addition to external projects and teachers enforcing ideological guidelines, gender ideology enters Italian schools through the introduction of the *carriera alias*, that is, the option for students to use a different name and identity. The spread of *carriera alias*, which began a few years ago, starting from universities and then quickly extending to high schools and middle schools, is nothing more than the application of self-ID.

At present there a number of schools, from north to south, that provide the opportunity to use the *carriera alias*,[60] which means that the identity declared by the student will have to be validated by everyone (teachers, students, school staff), resulting in the coercion to change one's language, and for girls to accept males entering their private female spaces and vice versa.[61] Anyone who

---

files/pub-pdf/ITGSE.pdf>.
60 The list of Italian schools with *carriera alias* can be found at <https://www.genderlens.org/carriera-alias/carriera-alias-elenco-scuole-italiane/>.
61 For school regulation on *carriera alias*, see <https://www.genderlens.org/regolamento-scolastico-per-la-carriera-alias/>.

dares to oppose this is immediately subjected to media bashing and accused of transphobia and discrimination, as happened in November 2022 to a teacher at a high school in Rome,[62] who refused to pretend that one of his female students was a male and for this was denigrated far and wide by the national press and prominent 'progressive' politicians and activists.

The role of mainstream media in silencing opposition to gender ideology is crucial. For several years, in fact, the press has been sponsoring *carriera alias* and 'genderless bathrooms' in schools at a rapid pace, describing these measures as "civil achievements" and as "steps forward on the path to rights," branding all forms of objection as medieval, bigoted and discriminatory. It is understandable that, in such a climate, all those teachers, principals and students who do not believe in 'gender identity' ideology are pushed to self-censor themselves in order not to be singled out as transphobic bigots—at best—or to suffer repercussions in their work and school careers—at worst.

It is because of the arrogant push from ideology-driven students themselves, often influenced by queer/LGBT/'trans'feminist activist groups, that principals introduce self-ID and 'gender-neutral bathrooms' in their schools, effectively forcing the entire school to participate in the social transition of trans-identified

---

[62] 'Prof rejects trans student's assignment: "In front of me there is a woman, not a man"'. *Roma-Corriere*. 10 November 2022. <https://roma.corriere.it/notizie/cronaca/22_novembre_09/roma-liceo-cavour-professore-si-rifiuta-applicare-carriera-alias-905d3a52-6054-11ed-8bc9-4c51e1976893.shtml?refresh_ce>.

students and to bow to the ideological dogma of 'gender identity', with practical consequences about freedom of expression and the right to privacy guaranteed by private spaces divided by sex.

Chapter 10

Child Transitions in Italy: The 'Debate' on Puberty Blockers[63]

Gender propaganda does not stop at schools.

Since early 2023, the mainstream press in particular has begun to focus rather aggressively on puberty blockers for so-called 'transgender kids'. The off-label use of blockers for gender dysphoria was authorised by AIFA (Italian Medicines Agency) in 2019, without much media trumpeting, but in January 2023, several articles and posts were published that described these drugs (which cause chemical castration and developmental blockade) as "life-saving"[64] and followed verbatim the 'transition or suicide' narrative that has been touted by international LGBTQ activists for nearly a decade now.

In particular, the rhetoric of suicide is leveraged—in pietistic and melodramatic tones—to convince the public of the need to

---

[63] To know more about child transitions abroad and in Italy, especially on puberty blockers: 'Child transitions (Part 1) From puberty blockers to medical transition'. *Il Mondo Nuovo* 2.0. <https://www.youtube.com/watch?v=9dGw5TyXb9o&t=2s>.

[64] 'Triptorelin for gender dysphoria in Italy, too: It's not a sex change and it saves lives'. *Wired*. 8 March, 2019. <https://www.wired.it/scienza/medicina/2019/03/08/triptorelina-disforia-genere/>.

medicalise those kids who were 'born in the wrong body', who would otherwise suffer the pains of hell. The most-read national newspapers feature headlines such as, "Puberty-blocking drugs, not guaranteeing them means denying help to those who need it"[65] and "Wrong to attack therapies, they saved our lives."[66] These articles describe the blockers—which are the same drugs used for chemical castration of sex offenders—as the only solution to save the lives of 'trans children'. Particular emphasis is placed on the bullying and discrimination suffered by these children, with the blatant aim of making the reader empathise to such an extent that he or she accepts the proposed solution—the pharmacological blocking of puberty—as the only and obvious choice. Anyone who dares to express doubts or opposition to the medicalisation of minors is labelled as reactionary, transphobic and conservative. This intellectually dishonest move is to associate dissent with a specific political faction, in this case the far-right.

Ignoring recent developments abroad, in Italy these drugs are still described as "safe and reversible" by the medical establishment and heavily promoted by activists, politicians, and the media apparatus. Pro-blocker propaganda reached its

---

[65] 'Puberty-blocking drugs, not guaranteeing them means denying help to those who need it'. *Il Fatto Quotidiano*. 24 January 2023. <https://www.ilfattoquotidiano.it/2023/01/24/farmaci-bloccanti-della-puberta-non-garantirli-vuol-dire-negare-un-aiuto-a-chi-ne-ha-bisogno/6941827/?utm_content=fattoquotidiano&utm_medium=social&utm_campaign=Echobox2021&utm_source=Facebook#Echobox=1674550271>.

[66] 'Wrong to attack therapies, they saved our lives'. *La Repubblica*. 19 January 2023. <https://www.repubblica.it/cronaca/2023/01/19/news/ragazzi_farmaci_bloccano_puberta-384171635/ >.

peak in the first weeks of 2023 following the stance taken by the Italian Psychoanalytic Society (SPI). Indeed, in a letter to Prime Minister Giorgia Meloni,[67] President Sarantis Thanopulos expressed the great concern of Italian psychoanalysts about the use of this treatment on minors and called for a rigorous scientific discussion of this matter.

In response, endocrinologists and paediatricians, as well as most journalists, were quick to publicly defend blockers and the affirmative approach. Endocrinologists, in particular, railed against the SPI position, which they believe risks creating "unwarranted alarm."[68] And they did so from a blatantly ideologically-driven position, arguing that psychological suffering in so-called dysphoric children stems from "the prejudice and stigma of those who deny that sexual identity can be incongruent with the sex assigned at birth." The refusal to acknowledge the pseudo-religious concept of 'gender identity/sexed soul' is belittled and stigmatised as the bearer of prejudice and stigma.

This is the same approach officially adopted, as early as the summer of 2022, by the Italian Society of Paediatrics (SIP), which in a public statement[69] openly endorsed the use of the affirmative

---

[67] 'Letter from the President of the Italian Psychoanalytic Society (SPI) to Prime Minister Giorgia Meloni'. January 2023. <https://feministpost.it/primo-piano/gli-psicanalisti-italiani-stop-ai-puberty-blockers/>.

[68] Endocrinologists respond to the letter of SPI: 'Allarme su bloccanti pubertà infondato, evitano suicidi e depressione'. *Adnkronos*. 20 January 2023. <https://www.adnkronos.com/endocrinologi-allarme-su-bloccanti-puberta-infondato-evitano-suicidi-e-depressione_3QgSEDT1yLVBSfQAJTyeCW>.

[69] 'The Italian Society of Paediatrics openly endorses the affirmative approach for gender dysphoric minors'. 4 August 2022. <https://sip.it/2022/08/04/accesso-

approach on minors, calling any attempt by a mental health professional to investigate other possible problems that might influence gender dysphoria gatekeeping and transphobia. In fact, according to Italian paediatricians, it is the 'stress of being denied the right to gender affirmation' that causes psychological suffering in these young kids, who should enjoy maximum autonomy in making irreversible decisions about their bodies, their fertility and their health.

According to accounts of parents of many of these trans-identified kids (the vast majority of whom are adolescent girls), the world of Italian psychologists is not far removed from the approach of endocrinologists and paediatricians. Most of these professionals, in other words, adopt the affirmative approach without question, immediately validating their young patients' stated 'identities' and setting them on the path to medical transition within a few months.

Getting a diagnosis of gender dysphoria, after all, is not that difficult, since diagnostic criteria[70] are mostly based on social—sexist—stereotypes of masculinity and femininity (preferences for certain clothes, games or activities). Moreover, the affirmative approach to 'gender identity' is advocated by most authoritative international medical societies, from the American Psychological Association to the American Endocrine Society, which in reality do nothing more than follow the—deeply ideological—guidelines

---

alle-cure-per-incongruenza-di-genere-modello-regionale-per-bambini-e-e-adolescenti/>.

70 'Dysphoria or social stereotypes? Guidelines for diagnosing gender dysphoria'. *Il Mondo Nuovo* 2.0. <https://www.youtube.com/watch?v=RtGgp4AQ5io>.

of the World Professional Association for Transgender Health (WPATH),[71] according to which the affirmative approach is the only one possible.

We are therefore in the presence of, in Italy as well as internationally, a medical class mostly devoted to blindly following the guidelines by the leading international medical authorities, putting obedience to the principle of authority before the care of their young patients. And, just as happens in other countries, most teachers, journalists and politicians conform, more or less consciously, to the doctrine of 'gender identity'.

---

71 WPATH—Standards of Care for the Health of Transgender and Gender Diverse People. Version 8 (Final version: 15 September 2022). <https://www.tandfonline.com/doi/pdf/10.1080/26895269.2022.2100644>.

Chapter 11

Dissenting Voices: The Italian Opposition to Gender Ideology

If, after many years, strong voices of opposition are beginning to rise in the English-speaking world, in Italy, resistance to the ideological colonisation of 'gender identity' is still very limited and, unfortunately, not at all cohesive.

Just as abroad, in fact, the two major anti-gender identity groups are represented on the one hand by radical feminism, including lesbian activists, and on the other by Catholic pro-life and pro-family proponents, two groups that are unlikely to be able to put aside their ideological differences to unite in defence of objective reality, women and children.

But, if we exclude these two groups and the fierce 'trans'feminist LGBTQ activism, the rest of the population remains largely unaware of the consequences that gender ideology has caused— and is still causing—in the rest of the western world and of the fierce public debate that has ensued.

The majority of Italians do not know about the phenomenon of child transitions, know nothing about the Tavistock scandal, and have no idea that in the United States 15-year-old girls (and even younger) can have their breasts amputated and obtain testosterone within a day without psychological therapy of any kind.[72] No Italian newspaper or news programme mentions the problem, raised in the United Kingdom by radical feminists, of men in women's prisons, nor is there any mention of the colonisation of women's sports by males in the United States.

Most of the Italian population does not even know about the dehumanising language imposed on women (menstruating people, uterus-havers, assigned female at birth, people with a front hole, etc.). As mentioned earlier, many people think homosexuality, transsexuality, transgenderism and transvestism are all the same thing. The concept of 'autogynephilia' (heterosexual men attracted to the idea of themselves as women)[73] and Blanchard[74]

---

72 'Chloe Cole, 18-year-old detransitioner speaks against child transitions'. *Il Mondo Nuovo* 2.0. <https://www.youtube.com/watch?v=L8UcOtltkpE&t=183s>.

73 'Are all trans women the same? Androphilia and autogynephilia'. *Il Mondo Nuovo* 2.0. <https://youtu.be/zKQCEuMD2R4>. See also Sheila Jeffreys. *Penile Imperialism: The Male Sex Right and Women's Subordination*. Mission Beach, Australia: Spinifex Press. 2022.
Michael Bailey. *The Man Who Would Be Queen: The Science of Gender-Bending and Transsexualism*. Washington D.C.: Joseph Henry Press. 2003.

74 Ray Blanchard et al. 'Heterosexual and homosexual gender dysphoria'. *Archives of Sexual Behavior* 16(2), pp. 139–52. 1987. <https://pubmed.ncbi.nlm.nih.gov/3592961/>; Ray Blanchard. 'The classification and labeling of nonhomosexual gender dysphorias'. *Archives of Sexual Behavior* 18(4), pp. 315–34. 1989. <https://pubmed.ncbi.nlm.nih.gov/2673136/>; Ray Blanchard. 'The concept of autogynephilia and the typology of male gender dysphoria'. *The Journal of Nervous and Mental Disease* 177(10), pp. 616–23. 1989. <https://pubmed.ncbi.nlm.nih.gov/2794988/>; Ray Blanchard. 'Clinical observations and systematic studies of autogynephilia'. *Journal of Sex and Marital Therapy* 17(4), pp. 235–51. 1991. <https://pubmed.ncbi.nlm.nih.gov/1815090/ >; Ray Blanchard. 'The she-male phenomenon and the concept of partial

and Lawrence's[75] research on this demographic is not popularised at all, especially by LGBTQ activists, who are careful not to acknowledge that under the 'trans umbrella', we can also find men who want to impose their paraphilia on society as a whole.

In addition to denying the existence of autogynephilia (and the influence of pornography on the development of trans identity in many autogynephiles[76]), transactivists also deny the existence of social contagion among children and young people.[77] And most Italians still hold in their minds the stereotypical idea of an MtF transsexual (a man with bottom surgery, attracted to men and engaged in prostitution), often overlapping this figure with that of a drag queen. Many still think that transsexuality (or transgenderism) is about a tiny portion of adult males who suffer because they are 'trapped in the wrong body', and nobody has a

---

autogynephilia'. *Journal of Sex and Marital Therapy*, 19(1), pp. 69–76. 1993. <https://pubmed.ncbi.nlm.nih.gov/8468711/>.

75 Anne Lawrence. 'Men trapped in men's bodies: Narratives of autogynephiliac transsexualism'. New York City: Springer Publishing. 2012; Anne Lawrence. 'Becoming what we love: Autogynephilic transsexualism conceptualized as an expression of romantic love'. *Perspectives in Biology and Medicine* 50(4), pp. 506–20. 2007. <https://pubmed.ncbi.nlm.nih.gov/17951885/>; Anne Lawrence. 'Shame and narcissistic rage in autogynephilic transsexualism'. *Archives of Sexual Behavior* 37(3), pp. 457–61. 2008. <https://pubmed.ncbi.nlm.nih.gov/18431633/>; Anne Lawrence. 'Autogynephilia: An underappreciated paraphilia'. *Advances in Psychosomatic Medicine* 31, pp. 35–48. 2011. <https://pubmed.ncbi.nlm.nih.gov/22005209/>.

76 'The influence of sissy porn on the transgender trend'. *Feminist Current*. 29 November 2020. <https://www.feministcurrent.com/2020/11/29/why-isnt-anyone-talking-about-the-influence-of-porn-on-the-trans-trend/>.

77 'ROGD (rapid onset gender dysphoria)—The explosion of transgenderism among teenage girls'. *Il Mondo Nuovo* 2.0. <https://www.youtube.com/watch?v=HbutUFAc8tw>.

Dissenting Voices: The Italian Opposition to Gender Ideology

clue that, in English-speaking countries, the phenomenon has reached exorbitant numbers especially among adolescent girls and young women, nor that the same trend is beginning to occur in Italy, as witnessed by several teachers and parents.

The voices of these concerned parents are not being heard by many. Only recently have their stories gained visibility on national television, but only at midnight, when the audience shrinks significantly. Late one night, an interview was aired with one of Italy's very first detransitioners, a 27-year-old man who identified for years as a so-called transgender woman and has now retraced his steps after removing his male genitals and having a vaginoplasty. In a 'normal' world, one would expect the story of a man convinced by medical professionals that he was a woman (the same professionals who would later castrate him) to make the front page of every newspaper. But the phenomenon of detransitioners[78] still remains largely ignored.

If the majority of Italians were exposed to the countless stories of detransitioning that one reads on Reddit and Twitter[79] and to the news about men in women's spaces and sports in other countries, much of the public would undoubtedly take a stand against gender ideology, against self-ID, and against the medicalisation of underage kids. LGBTQ activists know this very well, which is why they are so committed to introducing their ideological dogmas under colourful rainbow flags and masquerading it as a

---

78 'Detransitioners—Young people regretting their transition'. *Il Mondo Nuovo* 2.0. <https://www.youtube.com/watch?v=z-jQkoYHmUQ>.

79 REDDIT r/DETRANS. <https://www.reddit.com/r/detrans/ >; DETRANS UNITED: Support network for detransitioners <https://detransunited.com/>.

struggle for civil rights, freedom and self-determination, staking everything on the division between oppressed victims (anyone who identifies with the LGBTQIA+ alphabet groups), allies (the rest of the population, who must recognise their privilege and validate every demand of the oppressed) and evil oppressors (those who do not kowtow to the dogma).

Then again, only a monster could be against 'equal rights for all' and 'inclusion of the weakest'. Any opposition is immediately labelled as fascist, reactionary, medieval, transphobic, bigoted, TERF, and other epithets purposefully constructed to discredit and demonise the ideological opponent. In the US, transactivists even claim that a trans genocide is taking place because some states have banned sex transitions for those under the age of 18 in 2022 and 2023. This, in transactivist logic, is denying access to so-called 'gender affirmation care' (puberty blockers, hormones and surgeries) and an actual violation of human rights that will lead those who are 'denied the right to treatment' to take their own lives because of immense suffering.

One can see how, by changing the language to one's liking and shaping the way public opinion perceives reality turns out to be actually quite simple. And that is why, given the current state of affairs, informing the public about the extent of the phenomenon is the most valuable tool to counter its effects. If a parent is told that their child is participating in a project for minority inclusion against all forms of bullying, they will be unlikely to worry. But if that same parent knew that, behind all these fine words, their children are being taught that biological sex does not exist and that all human beings possess a gendered soul that can be dissociated from the body, resistance to this kind of 'education' would grow exponentially.

In Italy, as usual, Anglo-Saxon cultural phenomena arrive a few years later, which puts us in a situation of relative advantage, since by properly informing ourselves about what is happening abroad, we can avoid repeating the mistakes made elsewhere. In particular, if we are trying to counter an ideology such as 'gender identity'—which is promoted, as we know, primarily by mainstream institutions and the media—it is necessary to overcome any political and ideological differences.

This is not a 'right-wing' or 'left-wing' issue: this is about protecting objective material reality, freedom of thought and expression, and the rights of women and children. This is about restating the obvious, which is that men are men and women are women, a very simple truth, but one that gender ideologues consider the highest form of heresy.

This simple truth needs to be stated clearly and loudly: the more we reiterate it, the higher the chances of stemming the damage this disastrous ideology causes to individuals and society as a whole.[80]

---

[80] I thank Elisa Boscarol for her work on *The New World* 2.0 and writing chapters 8, 9, 10 and 11 of this book. I strongly suggest following her work. She is a scholar and populariser without any political and/or ideological affiliation. Her channel *Il Mondo Nuovo 2.0* is a project that she started in June 2022 on YouTube to distribute correct information on the ideology of 'gender identity' in Italy. The channel includes short informative videos and longer interviews with relevant people on the topic in question.

Chapter 12

The Tavistock and Portman Foundation: Its History at the Intersection of Psychiatry, Eugenics and Cybernetics[81]

The Tavistock and Portman Foundation in London was founded in 1921 as the psychiatric branch of the British Empire[82] that innovated psychiatric techniques through using mixtures of Pavlovian behaviourism and Freudian theories to influence behaviour. It has been funded to the tune of tens of billions of dollars over the past 50 years by the US government and in the 1930s and 1950s by the Rockefeller Foundation and the Macy Foundation, itself linked to the Rockefeller Foundation, which

---

81 This information comes from Matthew Ehret in 'How the Unthinkable Became Thinkable: Eric Lander, Julian Huxley and the Awakening of Sleeping Monsters'. <https://web.archive.org/web/20220823090327/https://expose-news.com/2022/03/01/how-the-unthinkable-became-thinkable/> and Daniel Estulin. *Tavistock Institute: Social Engineering the Masses*, Cesena: Trine Day LLC. 2015.
82 Daniel Estulin. *John Rawlings Rees. The Shaping of Psychiatry by War*. London and New York: W.W. Norton. 1945. See also Louise Marcus. 'The real CIA—The Rockefellers Fascist Establishment'. In *The Campaigner*. The Tavistock Grin. New York. April 1974. p. 6.

The Tavistock and Portman Foundation

was founded to support scientific investigations into fundamental aspects of health.

Both the Rockefeller and Macy Foundations funded and promoted eugenicist projects and research on 'race science'. They also funded research on 'psychosomatic interrelationships' to investigate how physiological changes affect the mind, from which they developed those psychiatric techniques that would later be called brainwashing.

After World War I, cases of so-called shell-shock were studied in the Tavistock clinic: how certain circumstances, such as intense combat stress, could induce substantial changes in an individual's personality. Beginning in the 1920s, the Tavistock Clinic was the main site for shell-shock research with an attempt to recreate the transformation of 'shell-shock trauma' outside the combat environment. Tavistock became the most important British research centre for psychological warfare.

During World War II, research developed on how to induce panic and how to disperse chemical and biological agents.

After the war, the Macy Foundation funded the creation of the World Federation for Mental Health (WFMH), and at the head of this new body we find Tavistock director John Rawlings Rees. Its purpose was to embed "psychiatric shock troops"[83] into every culture in the world.

Rees, in one of his strategic battle talks to reform society, said:

If we are going to prepare to come out and attack the social and national problems of our day, then we must have shock troops,

---

83 Daniel Estulin. Op.cit. Footnote 82, p. 12.

and these cannot be provided by psychiatry based entirely in institutions. We must have mobile teams of psychiatrists who are free to move around and make contact with the territory.

In 1947, the Tavistock Institute of Human Relations was created with funding from the Rockefeller Foundation. 'Transhumanist' eugenicist Julian Huxley—founder of the British Eugenics Society and the first director-general of UNESCO[84]—had also worked closely with the Tavistock Clinic and Canadian psychiatrist G. Brock Chisolm who had founded the World Health Organization (WHO) in 1948.

After World War II, the Macy Foundation organised conferences on cybernetics to create a model of a physiological system through which information is received from the environment, processed and then fed back to change that environment in order to control and influence the human mind itself. Thus,

---

84 Julian Huxley, the first director-general of UNESCO (United Nations Educational, Scientific and Cultural Organisation), in his 1946 document, *UNESCO: Its purpose and its philosophy*, explained the organisation's general objectives:

> [...] it will be important for UNESCO to see that the eugenic problem is examined with the greatest care, and that the public mind is informed of the issues at stake so that much that now is unthinkable may at least become thinkable. [...] It is, however, essential that eugenics should be brought entirely within the borders of science. [...] But in order to carry out its work, an organisation such as UNESCO needs not only a set of general aims and objects for itself, but also a working philosophy, a working hypothesis concerning human existence and its aims and objects, which will dictate, or at least indicate, a definite line of approach to its problems.

The term 'transhumanism' was coined in 1957 by Julian Huxley to describe his belief in the possibility of the transcendence of humankind.

the development of cybernetics—which since its origin has been concerned with real-time control and prediction of the phenomena and behaviours of living organisms in order to direct and modify them[85]—intersects with the Macy Foundation and Tavistock's research.

In order to change behaviour and intervene to affect it, the Tavistock psychiatrists were well aware that first it was necessary to change humanity's idea of itself by introducing a new idea of being human.

The ultimate goal of eugenicists and 'transhumanists' (transeugenicists), even today, remains the complete eradication of the sense of one's bodily identity, the tearing and subjugation of the deepest spirit of the human being, toward an erasure of the very sense of humanity. From the taking of bodies to the taking of the spirit and soul, we arrive at the ultimate siege of the human being, for everything is changeable, able to be transformed through technology to an identity of one's 'choice':

> The hopeless encirclement of man has been long in the preparation, through theories that strive for a logical and seamless explanation of the world and go hand in hand with technical development.[86]

It is thus no accident that clinics and research centres, such as the Tavistock, in their creation of the *universe* of meaning have come to deal with 'gender identity'.

---

85 For further information see Silvia Guerini and Costantino Ragusa. *5G: Rete della società cibernetica*. Trieste: Asterios Editore. 2021.
86 Ernst Jünger. *The Forest Passage*. Candor, NY: Telos Press Publishing. 2013.

Chapter 13

Trans Industry Attacking the Little Ones

The glittery trans industry is now attacking girls, boys and adolescents. The pressure exerted through social media, print and television and in every cultural sphere, especially in a progressive culture, is becoming stronger and stronger. New generations are the testing ground for the new world order, which is why it is so central to tear children away from families, to hand them over to technicians in white coats who will mould them according to the new transhuman dictates.

The 'gender identity' clinics and the large biomarket of identities sell synthetic illusions by creating a disassembly of bodies as a 'neutral' human being made sterile and ready for the laboratories of artificial reproduction.

In an episode of *Simply Naked*,[87] a Dutch public television programme, some transsexual adults show their naked bodies to ten to 12-year-old children. A little girl stares wide-eyed, looking confused. The host continues, asking a young man who identifies

---

87 "'Cambiare sesso è la felicità!'": La trans-industry spinge furiosamente sui bambini'. In *Feminist Post*. <https://feministpost.it/dal-mondo/cambiare-sesso-e-felicita-la-trans-industry-spinge-furiosamente-sui-bambini/?fbclid=IwAR3T HfwZWyd4zmw8HAnxlTS4vr7Yc9tMWDkDCnfBk-DLBtedbgAbr8S7H2Q>, accessed 24 April 2023.

as a woman, "What is a vaginoplasty?" The feminised-looking man replies that, "You surgically change the male sexual organ for the female sexual organ." As if that were really possible!

After explaining that there are not only males and females, but there is a whole 'spectrum' of gender identities, the host asks Anne Chris, a woman who had an elective double mastectomy: "How do you feel after the surgical operation?"

Anne Chris replies, addressing the children directly, "Do you know the word 'euphoria'? It means happy. Extremely happy. I woke up and my breasts were gone, I had the look I always wanted. Finally [my body] matched the way I felt inside. And I felt ecstatic."

"I mean, like how to fly?" asks a little girl.

"Yes!" Anne Chris replies with a big smile.

"You just feel intense happiness," the host intervenes.

"I want it too," concludes the little girl.

The boys and girls were asked for their impressions. A little girl replies that, "At first you think, huh? But later you realize that it's actually quite normal."

A little boy says that, "It's actually very normal."

In the name of promoting gender ideology—and the medical and pharmaceutical complex—girls and boys are put on television, exposed to naked 'trans-adults' and told that 'exhilaration' awaits them if they have their breasts and genitals mutilated. Wide-eyed children, at the prompting of adults, claim that this is "normal" and that "they want it too." Because what kid doesn't want to feel like he or she is flying?

"Changing sex is happiness!" This is what is transmitted: the trans industry furiously pushes its biotechnological tentacles on girls and boys.

"We can no longer remain silent on what appears to us to be serious abuse committed in the name of the emancipation of the 'transgender child,'" denounces a letter-appeal also signed by radical feminists such as Marie-Jo Bonnet, Nicole Athéa and Marie-Josèphe Devillers:

> ... an influence whose consequences lead to mental destabilisation, a break with the family if they do not support their child, and with all those who refuse to share their point of view. The speeches of these young people are often stereotyped as if they had lost all critical spirit [...] An abduction of childhood and a commodification of children's bodies. [...] This phenomenon, 'the transgender child' is a contemporary mystification that must be vigorously denounced because it is an ideological regimentation. They would have us believe that in the name of everyone's wellbeing and freedom, a child, relieved of the need for agreement with his/her 'reactionary' parents, would be able to 'choose' his/her so-called 'gender identity'. But the child is developing, his/her future is constantly evolving before reaching a stage of maturity. [...] Because by persuading these children that sex was 'assigned' to them at birth and that they can freely change it, we make them lifelong patients: lifelong consumers of hormonal chemical products marketed by pharmaceutical companies, consumers of ever more surgical operations in pursuit of the chimerical dream of a fantasised body.[88]

---

[88] 'Changement de sexe chez les enfants: "Nous ne pouvons plus nous taire face à une grave dérive"'.<https://www.lexpress.fr/actualite/idees-et-debats/

The Tavistock Clinic established the Gender Identity Development Service in 1989, specialising in the treatment of girls and boys with 'gender identity' problems.

A look at this clinic shows the approaches towards, and treatments of, girls, boys and adolescents, highlighting a complexity that cannot be reduced to empty slogans that often superficially and frivolously paint transitional pathways by placing them in a new paradigm in which fluidity and 'the neutral' become the new subversive subjectivities that disrupt heterosexual norms and binary logics.

The process of hormone treatment at the Tavistock Clinic could begin after only two meetings with specialists. From treating 80 patients in 2009, within ten years that number grew to almost 3,000 patients. Significantly, most of them were girls, and in 2012 it turned out that more than half of the girls were lesbians and almost half of the boys were homosexual.[89]

Feminist lesbian groups denounce a disappearance of lesbians:

> The Tavistock and Portman clinic [...] had become an assembly line where little butch lesbians in adolescent distress come in and FtMs

---

changement-de-sexe-chez-les-enfants-nous-ne-pouvons-plus-nous-taire-face-a-une-grave-derive_2158725.html, https://www.genethique.org/changement-de-sexe-chez-les-enfants-un-des-plus-grands-scandales-sanitaire-et-ethique/>, accessed 14 February 2022.

89 Transgender Trend. 'Is "affirmation" gay conversion therapy for children and young people?'. <https://www.transgendertrend.com/affirmation-gay-conversion-therapy-children-young-people/>, accessed 8 October 2021.

come out, with puberty blockers and referrals for irreversible life-changing surgeries.[90]

Thus, conversion therapies for lesbian girls were carried out regularly at the Tavistock. If we listen to the girls' stories, we understand how their discomfort with their changing bodies or their feelings toward other girls had not been recognised and understood, either by themselves, by their families, or by those psychologists who had pushed them toward puberty blockers, cross-sex hormones and surgeries. A lack of understanding of the self in a social context pushed these girls to say "if there is something different about me from other girls, then I am a man," rather than identifying as lesbians. In other words, an internalised homophobia leads lesbian girls to the path of 'transition'.[91]

At the Tavistock clinic, professionals provided 'gender self-affirmation-based care': when a boy, girl, or adolescent expressed what is seen as a desire to begin a path of transition, this intention was seen as definitive and was usually not questioned.[92] This model based on self-affirmation has been adopted in many countries. In 2018, the American Academy of Pediatrics issued a statement pointing to this very methodology for younger people as well. It is

---

90 Cristina Gramolini, Sabina Zenobi, Flavia Franceschini, Lucia Giansiracusa and Stella Zaltieri Pirola. *Noi, le lesbiche. Preferenza al femminile e critica al transfemminismo*. Milan: Il dito e La luna. 2021.
91 Marie-Jo Bonnet, Nicole Athéa. *Quand les filles deviennent des garçons*. Paris: Odile Jacob. 2023.
92 *Gli Orrori della Tavistock Clinic: Lo psichiatra David Bell rompe il silenzio*. In <https://feministpost.it/primo-piano/gli-orrori-della-tavistock-clinic-lo-psichiatra-david-bell-rompe-il-silenzio/>, accessed 22 April 2023.

the gender-affirming model developed in the 1990s by the Center of Expertise on Gender Dysphoria in Amsterdam, a model also known as 12-16-18, which at age 12 involves blocking puberty, at 16 the administration of hormones of the opposite sex, and at 18 surgical reassignment.[93] Of note is that mastectomy surgery referrals are increasing in England for 16- and 17-year-old girls.[94]

Puberty blockers were also given to children as young as ten years of age, a therapy that is almost always followed by synthetic opposite-sex hormones, which will need to be administered for life to sustain the so-called transition. The words of Dr Rachel Inker, who runs the Transgender Health Clinic at Community Health Centers in Burlington, USA, nicely highlight the trend toward narrowing the age range for accessing the entire transition pathway: "The choice to undergo surgery is a personal one that should be explored in every age group."[95]

Many children and adolescents who come to this and other clinics are victims of sexual abuse, parental abandonment, lesbo- or homophobia by family or schoolmates, or suffer from anorexia,

---

[93] For more information see Daniela Danna. *La piccola principe: Lettera aperta alle giovanissime su pubertà e transizione*. Milano: Vanda Edizioni. 2018.
Lisa Littman. 'Individuals Treated for Gender Dysphoria with Medical and/or Surgical Transition Who Subsequently Detransitioned: A Survey of 100 Detransitioners'. 2021. <https://link.springer.com/article/10.1007/s10508-021-02163-w>, accessed 6 November 2021; Maria Celeste. *Detransizione: Primo Studio Scientifico*. <https://feministpost.it/magazine/primo-piano/detransizione-primo-studio-scientifico/>.

[94] 'Scottish doctors approved breast removal for 51 trans teenagers'. *The Times Scotland*. 2021. <https://archive.is/zmz3d>, accessed 8 October, 2021.

[95] 'Vermont set to join handful of states in removing SRS minimum age for Medicaid recipients'. <https://4thwavenow.com/page/2/>.

bulimia, depression, anxiety, or autism.[96] These complicating factors and co-morbidities are often ignored and transition is considered the only solution. Instead of situating the problem in society, it is the *body* that is considered the problem, and gender ideology pushes adolescents to retreat into themselves, dwelling on their physical form—terrain where others have decided that it is their bodies that need to be transformed, thus causing them to lose sight of the *real* terrain of confrontation with the wider world where bodies reacting to abuse are able to recognise it:

> Postmodernists have argued that sex does not exist in itself, all is gender [...] Nevertheless, the medical interventions for 'gender dysphoria' are aimed at the minors' physical sex. This is the [postmodernist] 'original sin' of all this literature and all these interventions: if 'gender' substitutes 'sex', the body is excluded, and all that is left are the socially organised norms and perceptions of what is appropriate to one sex or the other.[97]

The intention of the gender-affirming model is the opposite of changing gender norms and making them less oppressive. This model aims instead to change the sex of 'eligible candidates' who suffer from society's disapproval of those who do not conform to sex stereotypes.[98]

---

96 Lisa Littman. Op.cit. Footnote 93.
97 Daniela Danna. 'Gender-affirming model still based on 2014 faulty Dutch study'. In *AG About Gender*. Vol. 10, No.19. 2021. <http://www.danieladanna.it/wordpress/minori-trans-tutto-e-basato-su-uno-studio-dalle-conclusioni-manipolate/>, accessed 8 October 2021.
98 Daniela Danna. Op.cit. Footnote 97.

The following are the words of a teacher who has worked for years with children and adults suffering from autism:

> Evidence is mounting that the relationship between the Trans Rights and Neurodiversity movements, which maybe initially seemed simpatico, benefits the former at the expense of the latter. Autistic women, especially lesbians, are being pushed out of their support networks. Autistic children whose behaviour does not fit gender stereotypes are being pathologised and medicalised. This is a conundrum the neurodiversity movement is going to have to grasp and soon. When disproportionate numbers of autistic people—children, even—are being diagnosed with gender dysphoria, the 'treatment' for which can lead to infertility, this starts to look worryingly like backdoor eugenics.[99]

To parents who are doubtful about the transition path, the pressure from doctors is strong: "Would you rather have a dead daughter than a live son?" leveraging alleged high risks of suicide. In fact, long-term studies (longer than ten years) show increases in suicide rates, psychiatric hospitalisation and lower quality of life *after* transition surgeries, not before:[100]

---

99 Christian Wilton-King. 'The Neurodiversity Movement's Toxic Relationship with Trans Rights Activism'. 2021. <https://www.transgendertrend.com/neurodiversity-movement-toxic-relationship-trans-rights-activism/>.

100 Dhejne *et al.*, 2011; Simonsen *et al.*, 2016; Kuhn *et al.*, 2009. More here: <https://www.transgendertrend.com/the-suicide-myth/>. accessed 8 October 2021.
Jennifer Bilek. 'Big Pharma Exploits and Monetizes "Trans Identity"'. In *The 11th Hour*. <https://www.the11thhourblog.com/post/big-pharma-exploits-and-monetizes-trans-identity>, accessed 24 October 2021.

> Ten to 15 years after surgical reassignment, the suicide rate of those who had undergone sex-reassignment surgery rose to 20 times that of comparable peers.[101]

The pressure on doctors is also strong, many of them denouncing the perennial danger of being labelled transphobic.

In a 2021 trial for damages against the Tavistock Clinic, in its defence the Clinic had young people who had begun the transition process testify. One of them was a 13-year-old teenager who stated that "he had no idea what he might think in the future about the possibility of having children" given that "he has never been in a romantic relationship the idea of having a child is something he is not considering right now."[102]

These words highlight how impossible it is for a child/young person to be able to give consent to procedures that he/she cannot yet understand, or to consent to ideological propaganda claims as a right for the self-determination of increasingly younger children. It is difficult to explain to children and girls what the loss of fertility or sexual function will mean for the future of many of them:

> I do not want any other young person who is distressed, confused, and lonely as I was to be driven to conclude transition is the only possible answer. I was an unhappy girl who needed help. Instead, I was treated like an experiment.[103]

---

101 Jennifer Bilek. Op.cit. Footnote 100.
102 Keira Bell. *Keira Bell: My Story*. <https://www.persuasion.community/p/keira-bell-y-story?r=7g6gd&utm_campaign=post&utm_medium=email&utm_source=twitter>, accessed 14 February 2022.
103 Keira Bell. Op.cit. Footnote 102.

These are the words of Keira Bell who won her case for damages against the Tavistock Clinic. Keira at age 16, after a series of very superficial conversations with social workers, was started on the transition path: she was prescribed puberty blockers, followed a year later by testosterone injections, and at age 20 she underwent a bilateral mastectomy.

The Appeals Court overturned the lower court's ruling, making the finding that it is up to doctors to take responsibility for deciding whether or not the minor possesses the maturity necessary to assess the consequences of hormone treatments. Transactivists rejoiced, but this case has forcefully opened a Pandora's box.

Psychiatrist David Bell, former president of the British Psychoanalytical Society, was the director of the Gender Identity Development Service (GIDS) at the Tavistock and Portman Clinic for more than 20 years. In 2018, he had compiled an internal report stating the concerns of many doctors at the Clinic about the way young patients, both girls and boys, were treated. Following this report, he was subjected to disciplinary action, which was followed by his resignation. Bell, now at the end of his career—as often happens among these 'repentant' scientists—describes the very serious damage caused by Tavistock to girls and boys, 40% of whom suffered from autism spectrum disorders. He declares that hormone therapies are in fact conversion therapies practiced on homosexual and lesbian minors, attributing strong responsibilities to LGBTQ + organisations, such as Stonewall and

Mermaids, which use the bodies of girls and boys for their own ends.[104]

In March 2023, the Gender Identity Development Service at the Tavistock and Portman clinic was closed. This decision by government order followed an interim report—the Cass Review—an independent evaluation of NHS treatments for children with gender dysphoria led by Dr Hilary Dawn Cass, former president of the Royal College of Paediatrics and Child Health and consultant in paediatric disability at St Thomas's Hospital in London. The interim report highlighted that "there is not enough evidence on the effectiveness of the affirmative model." It also reads: "Puberty blockers, rather than acting as a 'pause button' for children to explore their identities, appear to set them on a path to medicalised treatment."[105]

In an investigative book[106] on the Gender Identity Development Service of the Tavistock and Portman clinic, it emerged that most of the boys treated were on average 11 years old. In 2011, an "early intervention study" was undertaken to examine the effect of blockers on children under 16, because

---

104 Cathy Newman. "'Children have been very seriously damaged" by NHS gender clinic, says former Tavistock staff governor'. *Channel 4*. <https://www.channel4.com/news/children-have-been-very-seriously-damaged-by-nhs-gender-clinic-says-former-tavistock-staff-governor?fbclid=IwAR110kamqiYzJ2LuFLh9QPHFmJ38E74gr947PLWPgw8Kd04eAxEDRUR9JB8>, accessed 26 April 2023.

105 Independent review of gender identity services for children and young people. <https://sex-matters.org/posts/updates/the-cass-reviews-interim-report-is-out/>, accessed 26 April 2023.

106 Hanna Barnes. *Time to Think: The Inside Story of the Collapse of the Tavistock's Gender Service for Children*. London: Swift Press. 2023.

the effects on children were unknown. The GIDS had already eliminated all age limits for access to blockers in 2014, allowing children as young as nine to access them. At the same time, prescriptions were soaring, from 100 in 2009 to 2,500 in 2020, with another 4,600 boys and girls on the waiting list.

This book, *Time to Think* by Hanna Barnes, shows that past stories of sexual abuse were ignored: "In the case of a girl abused by a boy, I think one question to ask is whether there is any relationship between identifying as a boy and feeling safe." To every concern raised by doctors with their superiors they were always given the same answer: that children should be referred to be put on blockers unless they specifically said they didn't want them.

In addition, there were autistic or same-sex attracted children and adolescents. There were many cases of young people who had suffered homophobic bullying at school or at home and who then identified as 'trans'. In many cases, parents thought, "Thank God my child is trans and not gay or lesbian." The girls said, "When I hear the word 'lesbian' I cringe." When GIDS asked teens who turned to their service about their sexuality in 2012, over 90% of females and 80% of males said they were same-sex attracted or bisexual. Inside the clinic there was a macabre joke that "they weren't going to stay gay anymore at the rate GIDS was going."[107]

---

[107] Interview by Hadley Freeman. 'How the Tavistock gender clinic ran out of control'. In *The Times*. <https://www.thetimes.co.uk/article/tavistock-gender-clinic-puberty-blockers-nhs-investigation-fh7pngj0v>, accessed 26 April 2023.

In the United States, more than 1,000 parents from the Gender Forum in 2018 initiated a petition against the work of the American Academy of Pediatrics (AAP). They want a more careful evaluation to be put in place with respect to the affirmation approach:

> We parents know first-hand the results of the affirmation approach because many of our teens have been subjected to it. Many of our children were offered prescriptions after one or two doctor visits, or they were given a referral to a gender clinic to consult about transition after no attempt was made to explore other reasons for the sudden transgender claim. In many areas of the United States, it's no longer considered a matter of commonsense to question a sudden announcement of being 'born in the wrong body' in adolescence (with no previous signs), especially when preceded by or concurrent problem with anxiety, depression, autism, and/or questioning of sexual orientation.[108]

And in August 2021, a group of more than 3,000 pediatricians sued the Biden administration which, as a result of its reinterpretation of the Affordable Care Act, forces physicians to provide drugs and surgeries in transition pathways for minors.[109]

---

108 <https://4thwavenow.com/2018/10/29/parents-petition-american-academy-of-pediatrics-in-response-to-policy-statement-on-trans-identified-youth/>, accessed 7 October 2021.

109 <https://www.dailywire.com/news/3000-plus-pediatricians-medical-professionals-sue-biden-over-transgender-mandate>, accessed 26 April 2023. Translation adapted into Italian and published on *Feminist Post*: 'No to the transition obligation of minors thousands of US pediatricians are suing the Biden administration'. <https://feministpost.it/dal-mondo/no-

There is a growing number of countries moving away from drug treatment for *gender non-conforming* girls and boys and back to psychological interventions. Finland, Sweden, England and Norway have curbed the 'gender affirmative model'. For example, Finnish medical guidelines have been revised and now oppose the use of most puberty-blocking drugs and the transition of adolescents, but the transition pathway still remains possible for those cases considered *particularly severe* and, as we know well from the recent and past history of genetic engineering, the cases considered *severe* first act as a justification and later open up the whole process.[110]

These recent brakes on transeugenicist reality are positive but do not indicate that the whole transition industry is under threat or that the inherent risks of the treatments are being examined in depth. Medical guidelines and various bioethics committees have always followed the directions of pharmaceutical and biotechnology companies, and the signs of counter-trends could be read as a strategy until greater social acceptance for medical transition is gained, as well as the right moment to push even more forcefully in the direction already taken.

---

allobbligo-di-transizione-dei-minori-migliaia-di-pediatri-usa-fanno-causa-allamministrazione-biden/>, accessed 26 April 2023.

110 Finland Issues Strict Guidelines for Treating Gender Dysphoria. <https://genderreport.ca/finland-strict-guidelines-for-treating-gender-dysphoria/>, accessed 6 May 2023.

Chapter 14

The Transition of the Tavistock

In March 2023, the 'service for the development of gender identity' of the Tavistock and Portman clinic was closed, the only public facility open to minors. The service was closed due to a government measure. The services offered were deemed inadequate and the clinic was heavily criticised on the methods used to admit young patients. The outcome of this is that those who remain on the waiting list will be transferred to new regional services.

Evidently, the department had become too uncomfortable with Tavistock, especially after the case of Keira Bell who had brought the clinic to court for the speed with which it had started her on the irreversible transition path at the age of 16.

Does this closure really represent a change of gear? Unfortunately not, as the ground has been laid for the creation of greater social acceptance of transition in which psychologists will be able to affirm that they have done everything possible to understand the adolescent's discomfort and that the start of the transition path will represent his or her own will.

From now on, the NHS will transfer adolescents—turned into patients—from Tavistock to two new regional centres which will adopt a more rounded methodology which will take into account both physical and mental issues that cause problems. A further instrument includes research on decision making procedures.

Let us be clear, the administration of puberty blockers and subsequently of hormones of the opposite sex—which is equivalent to sterilisation—has not been stopped, and the surgical slaughter has not been stopped: all of this has merely been covered by a semblance of greater attention. Do we really think that adolescent discomforts, eating disorders, autism, psychological problems or homosexuality, lesbianism and behaviours that do not fit into stereotypes will be recognised? If clinics continue to churn out patients with so-called gender dysphoria, how can they liberate girls and boys, women and men, from gender roles without destroying bodies? Gender identity clinics will also continue to promote and reinforce stereotyped behaviour considering that adolescents and adults who go on the transition path must demonstrate that they possess those characteristics that, according to stereotypes, belong to the opposite sex.

It is also significant that, while we are reading this news, the Royal College of Obstetricians and Gynaecologists (RCOG) has published new guidelines on the "improvement of assistance for trans and people of different genders who access health services"[111] : Guidelines for the "preservation of fertility" for those accessing the transition path.

---

111 Draft guideline on the 'Care of Trans and Gender Diverse People within Obstetrics and Gynaecology' opens for consultation in the Royal College of Obstetricians and Gynecologists. <https://www.rcog.org.uk/news/draft-guideline-on-the-care-of-trans-and-gender-diverse-people-within-obstetrics-

These new guidelines highlight the need to inform those who undertake hormone therapy and surgery of their effects on fertility and of the possibility of accessing the cryopreservation of oocytes, sperm and ovarian or testicular tissues.

They also recommend that so-called trans men—that is, women—stop hormone treatment three months before trying to get pregnant. These guidelines, the first of many to follow, will inform the two new regional centres planned in London and the northwest of England to replace the Tavistock and Portman Clinic.

It is curious that, while they talk about new holistic approaches, they are in a hurry to give access to the cryopreservation of gametes to those who begin the transition path. This can only mean that they are preparing for an increase in such paths within a broader process of medicalisation—the engineering of bodies, and medically assisted procreation as the new normality of living. Evidently, all the big grants for gender policies that the pharmaceutical-biotechnological sector and the various philanthropic foundations have funded will have achieved what the donors expected.

The so-called holistic transition of Tavistock leads to the development of new centres extended throughout the country, which will be able to more widely enter into harmony with gender

---

and-gynaecology-opens-for-consultation/>, accessed 6 May 2023; UK's draft guideline for transgender care is published on the Society for Endocrinology's website. <https://www.endocrinology.org/news/item/18750/uk-s-draft-guideline-for-transgender-care-is-published>, accessed 6 May 2023.

policies that have already penetrated schools. Put differently, they will respond more quickly and more widely to the ever-increasing number of reports from psychologists in schools. It is therefore premature to rejoice about the closure of the Tavistock clinic.

Chapter 15

We Were Wrong

Some medicos pushed too hard to enable transition for minors and now they cannot keep silent about the consequences of puberty-blocking drugs and the constant testimonies of girls and boys who detransition.

"We were wrong," says Susan Bradley, a pioneer of puberty blockers:

> I admit the error and the damage, because their effects are serious and irreversible, because these treatments are authoritative and experimental, because in nine cases out of ten the 'dysphoria of gender' of children and adolescents is only temporary and masks other hardships, conditions or problems.[112]

Bradley is a leading Canadian psychiatrist and authority on gender dysphoria. She chaired the subcommittee on gender dysphoria for the fourth edition of the Diagnostic and Statistical

---

112 Story by Laurel Duggan. "'We Were Wrong": Pioneer in Child Gender Dysphoria Treatment Says Trans Medical Industry Is Harming Kids'. *The Daily Caller.* 11 March 2023. <https://www.msn.com/en-us/health/medical/we-were-wrong-pioneer-in-child-gender-dysphoria-treatment-says-trans-medical-industry-is-harming-kids/ar-AA18wUwy?ocid=msedgntp&cvid=e4f85cd7225f4c18b9d8a16cec>, accessed 6 May 2023.

Manual of Mental Disorders (DSM-IV), the official Manual of the American Psychiatric Association and had participated in the writing of the diagnostic guidelines for 'gender identity'.

In 1975, she founded the Clarke Institute of Toronto's Child Youth and Family Gender Identity Clinic (GIC), a paediatric clinic for children and adolescents diagnosed with 'gender dysphoria'. In this clinic they used an approach oriented towards psychological therapy and most of the children—transformed into patients undergoing psychotherapy—resolved the discomfort with their bodies and their biological sex:

> Around 2005, the Clinic began prescribing puberty-blocking drugs. We thought they were relatively safe and endocrinologists said their effects were reversible and we shouldn't worry. Deep down I felt that I was skeptical and felt that maybe we were making things worse and not helping them. And I think it's been confirmed that when these children start taking these drugs at any age, almost all of them end up wanting to switch to hormone therapy. [...] We were wrong. [...] They are not reversible as we have [always believed] and have long-term effects on the growth and development of children, which include infertility and a number of bone growth problems.[113]

In 2007, GIC was closed (following Bradley's retirement), under intense pressure from transgender activists who accused the clinic of being transphobic in that it did not automatically endorse the 'gender identity' as 'reported' by children.

Bradley says that almost all who were diagnosed with 'gender dysphoria' before the affirmative approach *overcame* their

---

113 Laurel Duggan. Op.cit. Footnote 112.

discomforts and accepted their body. Almost all of the boys, girls and adolescents who had turned to her clinic stopped believing that they were of the opposite sex over time. Bradley now believes that the majority of children and adolescents diagnosed with 'gender dysphoria' suffer from autism or autism spectrum personality disorders.

Autistic adolescents are prone to having issues with their physical appearance and have a hard time changing their minds once they are convinced that something is true, all of which make them more vulnerable to being convinced that they are of the opposite sex. Says Bradley:

> You have to put yourself in the shoes of a 12- or 13-year-old who thinks, 'This is my way of becoming normal' [...] These children are not doing well with today's affirmative approach. I don't know if there is a child who could do well, given the ability a 10, 12 or even 14 or 15-year-old has to understand the complexity of the choice he is making regarding his sexual function and his long-term life. It doesn't make any sense.[114]

Bradley thinks the transition is helpful for some adults and points out that some consider it the best thing they've ever done for themselves. But at the same time, she states that the metrics of success, including patient satisfaction, are actually quite complicated.

One of her patients who had made a "transition from woman to man," had married a woman who was a childhood friend of hers and seemed happy and satisfied, but later she underwent

---

114 Laurel Duggan. Op.cit. Footnote 112.

expensive phalloplasty surgery. Although she appeared "very masculine," the patient was never really satisfied and was always looking for further physical improvements.

Another patient Bradley had worked with had made a 'male-to-female transition', but 'she' eventually told psychiatrists that 'she' was no longer 'trans' and was in a relationship with another man. These and other experiences have made Bradley doubt that 'transition' for some people was just the search for a way to be accepted.

University Clinic Amsterdam UMC, a pioneer in the use of puberty blockers, has admitted that children on these drugs may find themselves locked into increased medicalisation. This admission comes following the publication of a new retrospective study examining 20 years of hormonal interventions known as the 'Dutch Protocol', conducted on more than 1500 children and adolescents between 1972 and 2018 at the famous Amsterdam Clinic and published in *The Journal of Sexual Medicine*.

However, this admission also comes after a report that revealed that the 2006 study on which the 'Dutch Protocol' and treatment with puberty blockers was based had been financed by Ferring Pharmaceuticals, the pharmaceutical multinational that markets triptorelin, the puberty blocker drug with which the natural development of girls and boys is stopped.[115]

---

115 Bernard Lane. 'One-way treatment. The famous Dutch clinic admits that puberty blockers may be a prediction, not a pause'. In *Gender Clinic News*. 30 January 2023. <https://genderclinicnews.substack.com/p/one-way-treatment?utm_source=post-email-title&publication_id=627677&post_id=99718464&isFreemail=true&utm_medium=email>, accessed 6 May 2023.

These methods are well known in the world of the pharmaceutical industry, where there is a pervasive control over scientific publications and their results, considering that the most important journals respond to interests linked to that sector. Also, safety and supervisory bodies are funded by money from pharmaceutical companies, with the routine mechanism of 'revolving doors' between researchers and top executives. Institutional policy is obviously not excluded: the transition from the management of pharmaceutical giants to managers in the public health sector allows for the approval of bills favourable to the pharmaceutical giants themselves. Healthcare executives and researchers are ready to return to cover new responsibilities in the pharmaceutical industry, once their contracts expire.

Rather than focus on the 'repentant psychiatrists' who have made their careers on the bodies of young people, I prefer to conclude with one of the many voices of the girls who have detransitioned. Luka Hein, in a video interview, takes us to the heart of the matter:

> [...] This is not the solution. Destroy my body, my life. I don't know what my future will be like. And I don't know my place in the world. There is no place for me. It's because of what was done to me, what I did to myself. I will never be a real male and at this point I can't even go back. And they'll tell you: 'it doesn't happen, no one does mastectomies on teenagers, it's all right, it's reversible, you can go back, you can do all of this'. What if you can't? It's called irreversible damage for a reason. Here I am now, at 20, wondering if I will

ever be able to have children, and hoping, praying that I haven't damaged myself irreversibly from that point of view.[116]

---

116 Luka Hein. 'La comunità trans mi ha mentito'. In *Il Mondo Nuovo 2.0*, <https://www.youtube.com/watch?v=vuxEdl0LkYI>, accessed 6 May 2023.

Chapter 16

An Experiment on Girls and Boys: The Consequences of Puberty Blockers and Cross-sex Hormones

Pushing a pause button on puberty is not possible. One must understand what blocking puberty entails. The administration of puberty blockers and subsequently of opposite-sex hormones, so called cross-sex hormones, constitutes real experimentation on children, especially girls, with irreversible consequences that are only gradually emerging. There is no doubt that more drastic consequences are still to be uncovered.

By way of illustration only, I will make a few references to this complex issue. Firstly, these treatments are sterilisations of girls and boys. Puberty blockers cause infertility, and those who take the transition path, if they later want to become parents, can only do so by resorting to artificial reproduction at MAP centres. Requests for cryopreservation of eggs and sperm before embarking on the transition path are increasing. If a girl or boy takes puberty blockers and subsequently cross-sex hormones at the age of 16, they will become infertile because their gametes (egg cells or sperm) have not been able to mature.

In addition to infertility, there are many other health consequences resulting from the use of puberty blockers, as sex hormones released at puberty are necessary for bone and brain development.

Gonadotropin Releasing Hormone (GnRH) analogues were first approved for use as drugs for end-stage prostate cancer in 1985 and are still widely used today. They are also prescribed for other purposes, including chemical castration for sex offenders in some states of the USA. These are the hormones used off-label as puberty blockers on children and are also used by women undergoing hormone therapy to suppress the production of their natural sex hormones, e.g. in IVF cycles.

The long-term adverse effects of puberty blockers impact psychological health, cognitive function and bone density. An effect now established as irreversible is bone demineralisation which leads to reduced growth in height and bone strength.[117] Numerous other pathologies in adulthood are expected to occur, such as obesity, diabetes, cardiovascular problems and psychological problems.

Suffice to say that a 2017 study of men with prostate cancer undergoing treatment with GnRH analogues showed that the treatment affected cognitive function, including language ability and short-term memory capacity.

---

117 Polly Carmichael *et al.* 'Short-term outcomes of pubertal suppression in a selected cohort of 12 to 15 year old young people with persistent gender dysphoria in the UK'. In *Plos On.* <https://journals.plos.org/plosone/article?id=10.1371/journal.pone.0243894>, accessed 20 April 2023.

In the United States, a GnRH analogue drug (with the trade name Lupron) was approved in 1993 for use in children affected by early-onset puberty and was also commonly used off-label in children with excessive growth patterns. Studies have shown that girls who received Lupron therapy developed serious problems such as bone thinning and haematological and joint problems as adults.

As for cross-sex hormones, these also have serious irreversible effects, even when treatment to counter the side-effects is introduced.[118] In Janice Raymond's words:

> Transgender activists champion the 'right' to hormones and surgery for every child who presents as 'dysphoric', treatments they define as 'emergency medical care'. This rhetoric of dysphoria allows accusers to assert that opponents are depriving children of necessary health care, as if hormones are an issue of life and death comparable to insulin needed by those with diabetes. […] Instead of supporting a child's right to protection from the health risks of such procedures, trans activists claim that robbing children of quick affirmation of treatment is life-threatening and may cause suicide.
>
> The suicide alarm is used as a cudgel to hammer trans tenets into truths. Suicide numbers are blown out of proportion and invoked widely within trans circles, especially to defend certain medical procedures for young people.[119]

---

[118] Some information I used for this chapter, and much more, can be found here: 'The Tavistock's experimentation with puberty blockers: the effects on bone density'. 2021. <https://www.transgendertrend.com/puberty-blockers/>, accessed 8 October 2021;

[119] Janice G. Raymond. *Doublethink: A Feminist Challenge to Transgenderism*. Mission Beach: Spinifex Press. 2021, pp. 223–224.

Chapter 17

No Girl or Boy is 'Born in the Wrong Body'

In the face of distress that can have multiple causes and manifestations, it is asserted that boys and girls are *born in the wrong body*. Eating disorders, autism, depression, adolescent discomfort, homosexual and lesbian behaviours that do not fit stereotypes are no longer taken into account.[120] They fade away and are transformed into what is called *gender dysphoria*, a diagnosis that did not exist before 2013, the year in which it was introduced in the fifth edition of the Diagnostic and Statistical Manual of Mental Disorders (DSM-V).[121] This passage in itself amounts to a pathologisation and a medicalisation:

> The diagnosis of 'gender dysphoria' in boys and girls, in addition to the characteristics required for all ages, marked incongruity between birth sex and perceived 'gender identity' (identification with the opposite gender), which has been present for at least six

---

120 Lisa Littman. Op.cit. Footnote 93.
121 Gender Dysphoria Diagnosis. In *American Psychiatric Association*. <https://www.psychiatry.org/psychiatrists/diversity/education/transgender-and-gender-nonconforming-patients/gender-dysphoria-diagnosis>, accessed 6 May 2023.

months; clinically significant distress or functional impairment resulting from this incongruence) requires at least six of the following characteristics:
- a strong desire to belong or an urge to be of the other gender (or some other gender);
- a strong preference for dressing in typical clothes of the opposite sex and, in girls, resistance to wearing typical female clothing;
- a strong preference for switching gender roles when playing games;
- a strong preference for toys, games, and activities typical of the other gender;
- a strong preference for playmates of other genders;
- a strong rejection of toys, games and activities typical of the gender that corresponds to the birth sex;
- a strong aversion to their anatomy;
- a strong desire for primary and/or secondary sexed characteristics that correspond to perceived 'gender identity'.[122]

It does not take much to read through these criteria to understand how steeped in sexist stereotypes they are and how many adults, if they were girls and boys today, would be defined as 'dysphoric'.

The new approach of *gender affirmation* pushes girls and boys down a path that involves irreversible medical and surgical interventions. But no girl and no boy is *born in the wrong body*. Adults should try to understand how varied human behaviours and preferences can be; they should understand that both

---
122 Disforia di genere. In *Manuale MSD*. <https://www.msdmanuals.com/it-it/professionale/disturbi-psichiatrici/sessualit%C3%A0-disforia-di-genere-e-parafilie/disforia-di-genere>, accessed 27 April 2023.

being male and being female have a wide range of personalities, preferences and possibilities.

To the rhetoric used to justify the administration of puberty blockers to allow us to 'have time', I reply that it is the exact opposite: it is precisely the blockers that prevent physiological maturation, sexual development and a clearer self-understanding. The puberty process is stopped.

This is a medicalisation, an experimentation on girls and boys marketed as a claim for freedom by the LGBTQ+ movement. But as I wrote in 2018:

> It is for the free choice of the girl child, we are told, but blocking puberty does not promote the choice of the girl child: it is us who implement a choice and a very specific one. Is there not a risk that such an approach goes to reconfirm and reinforce the very gender stereotypes that should be broken down? A little girl who does not fit into the socially accepted characteristics and behaviours that her sex 'should' have—so that she is not what we imagine as 'feminine'—and who plays games that do not fit into those labelled as 'girlish', or who shows an interest in other little girls, is seen as a boy and not as a little girl who does not fit the stereotype. It is a feeling, a behaviour, a tension that is trapped. These need to be liberated, not by implementing medicalisation on girls, but by opening up the society that labels such feeling, and behaviours as 'outside the norm', in relation to the socially constructed gender. *We should not erase bodies to get rid of genders, but we should liberate bodies from genders.*[123]

---

123 Silvia Guerini. 'La Metamorfosi del mondo'. In *L'Urlo della Terra*, Numero 6, July 2018. <https://www.resistenzealnanomondo.org/necrotecnologie/la-

At Castleview Primary School in Edinburgh, Scotland, in a recent initiative aimed at 'promoting equality', male teachers and male pupils were asked to go to school wearing a skirt. An initiative that actually confirms the same stereotypes.

"Let kids just be kids," denounce the parents. "If a male wants to wear a skirt he should be free to do so, but why pressure others and ask them to do the same thing?" wonders one father of a child.

In many US states, silicone penises sized for girls under the age of five are available for free, to be tucked into shorts to simulate male genitalia. This penis is recommended for girls with *noncompliant* behaviours. And in a British school, a newsletter to "inform, promote and raise awareness about LGBTQ+ issues" teaches 11-year-old girls how to bind their breasts while waiting to have them removed.[124] These may seem like extreme and marginal examples, but they are representative of a trend that is expanding beyond all recognition.

---

metamorfosi-del-mondo/>, accessed 14 February 2022.

124 Sophie Tanno. 'Sixth-formers at top grammar school send newsletter to girls as young as 11 detailing how to bind their breasts to "look more masculine" and how surgery can remove tissue if it hurts too much'. In *MailOnline*. 2021. <https://www.dailymail.co.uk/news/article-9558773/Sixth-formers-grammar-school-tell-girls-bind-breasts.html>, accessed 22 April 2023.

Chapter 18

A Broader Reflection on Transsexualism, Transition Pathways, and Their Rise

Historically, while some people who felt *trapped* in their black skin were sold skin lightening creams for the purpose of 'pigmentation change', this did not ever become a mainstream medical practice. Eventually, it was recognised that such feelings of being trapped were encouraged by a society that oppressed and discriminated against people because of their skin colour and that it was society that needed to be changed, not the individual.

Here I refer to the analysis of feminist Janice G. Raymond, who said that:

> I believe that the *First Cause*, that which sets other causes of transsexualism in motion (such as family stereotypes and interactions), is a patriarchal society, which generates norms of masculinity and femininity.[125]

---

125 Janice G. Raymond. *The Transsexual Empire: The Making of the She-Male.* Boston: Beacon Press. 1979, p. 70.

From the 'Neutral' Body to the Posthuman Cyborg

This makes me pause and reflect about people who believe they are 'transgender' who are not at all encouraged to consider this feeling as stemming from social constraints that define feminine or masculine behaviours and their respective roles. This reflection of mine is not meant to deny the discomfort that some people feel with their bodies, but it is meant to open a deeper and more complex reflection on transgenderism, transsexualism, transition practices and their rise.

A girl or boy, a teenager, a woman or a man, who does not fit the stereotypes is encouraged to think of herself or himself as *born in a wrong body* and not as an individual who is trying to get out of imposed roles:

> ... there would be less need for injurious body modifications, including hormone treatment, mastectomies, and penectomies, if the trans canopy had not become the reference point for what is actually sex role dissatisfaction and gender non-conformity.
>
> Trans advocates have no monopoly on gender non-conformity. Why should gender non-conforming behavior be confined to the realm of transgender and turned into an object of medical attention? Transgenderism depoliticizes non-compliant behavior and restricts it to a so-called gender identity, thus making it a question of individual behavior amenable to hormone treatments, surgery and self-identification. Clinicians should be encouraging young people to challenge sex roles without rejecting their natal bodies.
>
> Gender non-conformity is just what it says—the practice of not conforming to role-defined rules and regulations, no matter whether they are traditionally or progressively presented. People

shouldn't need to identify as transgender or transsexual to live a gender non-compliant life.[126]

The classification of transsexualism as a therapeutic category also inserts non-stereotypical behaviour into a medical paradigm that will implement a political and social structuring of what should be masculine and feminine behaviour. 'Gender identity' clinics promote and reinforce stereotypical behaviour. For example, for men who want to embark on the path of transition, a primary requirement is that they possess and are able to demonstrate those characteristics that, according to sexist stereotypes, belong to women, from dress deemed socially feminine to body language.

Medicalising suffering related to stereotypes puts the individual in the hands of the medical and pharmaceutical system, and thus, instead of changing the structures of society, those individuals who do not fit the stereotypes will *receive treatment*.[127]

"Medicine focuses on the surgical construction of desired genitalia. Artefacts of silicone breasts, artificial vaginas come to embody what is considered the essence of femininity."[128] The overall result of these surgical treatments is that the 'transsexual' becomes a participant in a society that encourages conformity to stereotypes, and the medical solution becomes a social tranquiliser.

---

126 Janice G. Raymond. *Doublethink: A Feminist Challenge to Transgenderism*. Mission Beach, Australia: Spinifex Press. 2021, pp. 225–226.
127 Collectif anti-genre. 'Transgenrisme, effacement politique du sexe et capitalisme'. 2021. <https://www.partage-le.com/2021/05/03/transgenrisme-effacement-politique-du-sexe-et-capitalisme-par-le-collectif-anti-genre/>.
128 Collectif anti-genre. Op.cit. Footnote 127.

From the 'Neutral' Body to the Posthuman Cyborg

Transsexual surgery also enables physicians to gain medical knowledge about the manipulation of human sexuality that probably could not be gained from other medical procedures.[129] This brings to mind sad historical periods when any kind of human vivisection was possible. We know that, when Nazism came to an end, those scientists—or that knowledge—were coveted all over the world in the most prestigious research centres. Can we be so sure they are not forcing situations or creating them inappropriately so that new opportunities for experimentation are made available? As Jennifer Bilek comments:

> With improvements in plastics initially used in surgeries in the early 1900s to reconstruct the atrocious damage to those injured in war, the use of these plastics has blossomed into a cosmetic industry of chosen body modifications worth nearly $17 billion annually. Causing harm to the human body for image enhancement to align with one's self-chosen ideal has become more and more popular. With advancements in technology, artificial intelligence, and an eye toward moulding humans more closely with technology and AI, the medical ethic of 'first do no harm' is being shifted even more to accommodate these changes, until finally, we may see it disappear altogether as a solid principle of protection humans.
>
> Transsexualism, up until the past decade, was a medical disorder, needing strict psychiatric and physician oversight to weigh the cost of harm to the human body incurred to alleviate the psychological suffering of patients. In the past two decades, it has

---

[129] Janice G. Raymond. 'Technology on the Social and Ethical Aspects of Transsexual Surgery'. Paper prepared for the National Center for Health Care Technology, US Department of Health and Human Services. 1980.

quickly morphed into a new realm of 'identity medicine', driven by elites heavily invested in the medical-industrial complex. In this new realm, the ethic of 'first do no harm' is further stretched to help actualize individual identities as they relate to the sexed body, overlaid with cultural sex-role stereotypes.

Transsexualism has been rebranded transgenderism for marketing purposes and is being sold to young people as if it were a new fashion line. The harm incurred to the human body is seen, in this new realm of 'identity medicine', as subordinate to any psychic pain or emotional discomfort the individual suffers from, which may simply be their desire for self-actualization. With these changes, greater and greater harms to the human body are being justified, medical ethics stretched beyond imagining, for an ideal body that reflects each person's imagination.[130]

The Align Surgical Associates Clinic in San Francisco offers three new genital combinations to those who feel simultaneously male and female or completely neutral. Composable and decomposable genitality is the latest approach.

Surgery for girls, in particular, is on the rise as they embark on a path of transition. But their subsequent detransitions are also on the rise. The testimonies of these girls and young women reveal a demand for understanding that is deeply social and does not need a technical-medical response. Girls are often influenced

---

[130] Jennifer Bilek. 'Queering Medical Ethics Toward a Profiteering Model of Human Body Mutilation'. In *The 11th Hour*. March 2021. <https://www.the11thhourblog.com/post/queering-medical-ethics-toward-a-profiteering-model-of-human-body-mutilation>, accessed 2 October 2021.

by social media activists who advocate transition as the only solution to their difficulties. Here is one of many testimonies:

> Many people on the blogs I frequented described feeling trapped in their body and uncomfortable in their skin; they described being unhappy with their breasts and their hips, and feeling unattractive. On these blogs, these feelings were considered symptoms of gender dysphoria, and a sure sign that transitioning to the opposite sex with the help of hormone treatment and invasive surgery was the right course of action. At no point were negative side effects of these procedures discussed, nor was the possibility considered that these feelings might not be related to gender in the first place. At this age, there was much I disliked about my body, and combined with my need to reject traditional femininity, it seemed logical that gender dysphoria was the explanation for these feelings. I now had a way to experience self-expression and reject stereotypical femininity with male haircuts and clothes, and the term gender dysphoria to explain my body insecurities. […] After this, it wasn't difficult for me to convince myself that transitioning was the key to happiness and security. I believe this might be the case for other young people claiming to experience gender dysphoria: obsession with gender serves as a way to avoid dealing with more complex, underlying issues with confidence, identity and security. These need to be dealt with first, before transition can even be considered.[131]

---

131 Juliette van Steensel. 'Finding middle ground: The importance of empathy'. <https://4thwavenow.com/2019/10/05/finding-middle-ground-the-importance-of-empathy/>, accessed 5 October 2019.

A Broader Reflection on Transsexualism, Transition Pathways, and Their Rise

The world of social networking, which promotes transition as an easy and appealing recipe for solving other problems, is pushing more and more young people toward trans-identification. The first *transgender superheroine* who featured in Disney's Marvel Comics series *Marvel's Hero Project*[132] is a 12-year-old with long pink hair and a young LGBTQ+ activist who began the transition journey at age eight: "Being a transgender activist at 13 is almost like having superpowers."[133] These words resonate like an ad-hoc pre-packaged commercial. The castration of children has been turned into entertainment on social networks and reality TV—"Jazz Jennings prepares for gender confirmation surgery with a 'Goodbye Penis' party"[134]—with young stars literally thrown into a meat grinder and teenagers fascinated by these stories that sweeten and mystify reality to normalise surgical butchery and sterilisation.

Young people who, in the solitude into which they are plunged, perpetually in front of a screen, are less and less able to cope with normal adolescent challenges combined with increasing discomfort toward their own bodies, relational difficulties, and psychological fragility. Trans-identification offers an apparent

---

132 <https://www.rebekahbruesehoff.com/>.
133 <https://www.elle.com/it/magazine/women-in-society/a30993571/rebekah-bruesehoff-attivista-transgender/>.
134 Jennifer Bilek. "'Gender Identity" The Techno Medical Complex and Twerking Men in Monkey Suits'. In *The 11th Hour*. August 2021. <https://www.the11thhourblog.com/post/gender-identity-the-techno-medical-complex-and-twerking-men-in-monkey-suits>, accessed 25 November 2021.

and illusory way out of one's difficulties along with a completely new identity through the modification of one's body. Herein lies the central node and bridge to so-called 'transhumanism' that I will address in the conclusion of this book.

Chapter 19

Not Wanting to Be a Woman: The Link between Anorexia and Trans-Identification

As far as adolescents are concerned, we are faced with a real social contagion towards trans-identification. In addition, so-called 'rapid onset gender dysphoria' (ROGD)[135] is spreading, involving above all post-pubertal girls who suddenly declare that they do not identify with their sex. The unusual fact is that this also occurs in groups of friends in which most or even all members of the group come to no longer identify as female. If we listen to the testimonies of the parents,[136] it emerges that these adolescents and young adults were totally immersed in social networks and when they later began to have new friendships or

---

135 Lisa Littman. 'Rapid Onset of Gender Dysphoria in Adolescents and Young Adults: A Descriptive Study'. In *Journal of Adolescent Health* 60(2:1). 2017. <https://www.jahonline.org/article/S1054-139X(16)30765-0/fulltext>, accessed 27 April 2023.

136 Lisa Littman. 'Parent reports of adolescents and young adults perceived to show signs of rapid onset of gender dysphoria'. In *PLOS ONE* (13:8). 2018. <https://journals.plos.org/plosone/article?id=10.1371/journal.pone.0202330>, accessed 27 April 2023 and <https://www.ipetitions.com/petition/brown-university-and-plos-one-defend-academic>, accessed 27 April 2023.

to have romantic relationships outside the grip and dependence of social networks, they returned to recognising themselves as their own sex.

A thread connects the social contagion among members of a group with regard to the appearance of eating disorders and, specifically, of anorexia, and the social contagion with regard to the appearance of 'rapid onset gender dysphoria'.[137] A concern about one's body and image caused by 'excess pounds' is created, self-reinforced, and reinforced by others, as are concerns about one's body and image that are perceived to be caused by one's natal sex. In the first case, the solution is to lose weight to the extreme, while in the second, to try to cancel one's sex through the 'transition' path. In both cases it is a destruction of one's body.

Anorexia can be interpreted as the desperate search for a perfect physical form which underlies an objectification of the female body according to certain standards of thinness. But it could also be interpreted as an extreme refusal of precisely that objectification of the body and an extreme refusal of sexual development, and of a female body that tends towards an androgynous or 'neutral' body. Menstruation is interrupted; the embodied bond that passes through our blood is interrupted.

The connection between eating disorders and trans-identification is deeper than it may seem. In the years immediately following puberty, young women are more vulnerable and

---

[137] Eliza Mondegreen. 'Trans Identification and Eating Disorders'. In *Genspect*. 23 October 2022. <https://genspect.org/trans-identification-and-eating-disorders/>, accessed 22 April 2023.

insecure about their bodies and sexuality. In the case of eating disorders, extreme self-doubt can lead them to want to deny their bodies by stopping eating. In the case of so-called 'rapid-onset gender dysphoria', girls wage war on their own bodies by destroying them with hormones and surgery.

It is self-harm, a hatred towards your body that you don't accept because, basically, you do not want to be a woman. It is once again the female and maternal body that becomes a battlefield as it has been for some time in transhumanist appropriation, re-signification, cancellation and artificialisation.

A profound testimony brings us back to the meaning of these processes of negation of the body:

> The fear isn't becoming fat so much as becoming flesh. The anorexic persecutes the body that betrays 'the self' by its very existence: by its femaleness, by its soft curves and dark secrets, by blood, by the reproductive potential written into female flesh and by the things society writes on that flesh. Anorexics aspire to be pure spirit, pure intellect. They need only one food: not to violate the 'self' by becoming flesh. Transition, too, scapegoats the body for its failure to faithfully represent 'the self'. Gender-dysphoric people talk about feeling like a 'brain in a jar' or a gender identity stuck in a 'meat vehicle' or 'flesh suit'. Major surgeries are spoken about with cool disregard, as though they were minor home-remodeling projects. [...] On the altar of passing, clinicians and patients sacrifice health and function. If transition is about becoming your true self, why is there so little focus on being, and so much focus on appearing, seeming, passing, and pretending? Why edit the past, rather than own it? Why cut out organs and discipline natural gestures? No,

> something else is going on here: the pathological exercise of control over a body alienated from the self.[138]

Unlike anorexia and other eating disorders, trans-identification is glorified and sold as a liberating process. But now we are even witnessing a disavowal of eating disorders and psychological and adolescent discomforts that are re-signified and therefore diagnosed as 'gender dysphoria', transformed into a new synthetic identity, a dissociation from one's sexed body and a claim to new rights bestowed by a progressive, rainbow and transgenic left together with LGBTQ+ organisations and the pharmaceutical and bionanotechnological apparatus.

This is linked to a reflection on the phenomenon of transition which has changed profoundly over the last 30 years because today more women than men and, specifically, more girls, undertake it. As Marina Terragni has said:

> Once FtMs, from female to male, were an absolute rarity. The proportions were roughly one FtM [for] every hundred MtF, and even then they were two anthropologically different and distant worlds. Today FtMs constitute the clear majority of early transitions—7-8 cases out of 10—and the interpretation criteria need to be updated.
>
> An important difference: while recourse to hormonal therapies and surgery –castration—is increasingly rare among MtFs in favor of self-identification that keeps the body intact [self-ID], FtMs very frequently resort to chemical support and double mastectomy

---

138 Eliza Mondegreen. Op.cit. Footnote 137.

[called] top surgery (much less frequently to the construction of a pseudo-male [construction of penis]).

Symbolically, however, both types of transition tell the same story. It is always a matter of erasing the body. In the case of FtMs, it is a real escape from the destiny of being women, understood as disempowerment, loss of freedom, renunciation, subordination, misery. The movement is the same as—at a later stage—of the anorexic. As the detransitioners often say, it's more about stopping the process of becoming a woman, with all that follows, than being a man.

In the case of MtFs, instead, it is a question of replacing biological women with their own 'new' bodies of pseudo-women, autogynephilically and cosmetically reconstructed, according to the canons that are linked to the most ingrained gender stereotypes, or by indulging the pretensions of the male gaze.[139]

If anorexic adolescent girls were treated in the same way as girls who want to begin the transition path, they would not be encouraged to change their relationship with food, with their bodies, with themselves, but they would be told to believe they were right in thinking they were fat, and that their true innate self is thin. Maria Terragni continues:

... feeling as perpetually 'fat', wanting to become more and more 'thin', as well as feeling of the opposite sex, of no gender, of a fluid, neutral state, represents the need to be different from how one is. For teenage girls the fear is of growing up and being a woman.

---

139 Marina Terragni. 'Le due facce della transizione oggi'. 27 July 2021. In *Feminist Post*. <https://feministpost.it/varie/ftm-e-mtf-le-due-facce-della-transizione-oggi/ >, accessed 24 April 2023.

Anorexia and trans-identification are both rooted in the belief that by changing one's body one will no longer hate oneself. Both confuse self-annulment with liberation; both desperately follow an escape route from the reality of bodies.

Chapter 20

Gender Ideology and Paedophilia

The normalisation of paedophilia has been an ongoing process for some time. Alfred Kinsey, a US biologist, made a career as a sexologist in the 1950s by publishing the famous and controversial Kinsey reports on the sexual behaviour of human beings—*Sexual Behaviour in the Human Male* and *Sexual Behaviour in the Human Female*—at the conclusion of his research. The research was funded by the Rockefeller Foundation beginning in 1940.[140]

In these reports, Kinsey illustrated the results of 'experiments' on the sexuality of boys and girls to demonstrate their ability to experience an orgasm. A British documentary, *Kinsey's Paedophiles*, highlights how these 'experiments' were the result of sexual abuse of boys and girls, as reported by paedophiles.[141] In the 1990s, John Bancroft, director of the Kinsey Institute, admitted that the data in the reports were based on the personal experiences of a sex offender who had molested more than 300 children and kept an accurate diary of his experiences.[142]

---

[140] Enrica Perucchietti and Gianluca Marletta. *Unisex*. Bologna: Arianna Editrice. 2015.

[141] <https://it.wikipedia.org/wiki/Rapporti_Kinsey#Sessualit%C3%A0_infantile>.

[142] <https://ricerca.repubblica.it/repubblica/archivio/repubblica/1995/12/09/le-memorie-di-un-pedofilo-nel-rapporto.html>.

According to Kinsey,

> the problem of paedophilia would be a false problem, since there would be no danger of corrupting the innocence of childhood, which so repulses consciences, because this innocence would be only one of many invented myths.

He continued with, "It is difficult to see why a child, unless conditioned by upbringing, should be upset when her genitals are touched."[143]

John Money began to whitewash paedophilia by arguing that there must be a clinical distinction between 'affectional pedophilia' in which there is affection for the child involved in sexual acts, and 'sadistic pedophilia', which manifests itself only in a sadistic way.[144] Money, in the preface to the book *Boys on Their Contacts with Men*, states that "pedophilia and ephebophilia are not a voluntary choice. [...] One must simply accept that they exist."[145]

Links between the LGBTQ+ movement and associations defending paedophilia include the fact that in the 1980s, the North American Man/Boy Love Association (NAMBLA), which opposed legislation banning sexual relations between adult men and minors, joined the International Lesbian and Gay Association (ILGA).

---

143 Enrica Perucchietti and Gianluca Marletta. Op.cit. Footnote 140.
144 <https://www.documentazione.info/la-storia-del-dottor-john-money-il-caso-dei-gemelli-bruce-e-brian-reimer-e-la-teoria-del-gender> and <https://it.wikipedia.org/wiki/John_Money>.
145 Theo Sandfort. *Boys on Their Contacts with Men: A Study of Sexually Expressed Friendships*. Goa, India: Global Academic Publishers. 1987.

It issued the following demand:

> NAMBLA ... calls for the adoption of laws that both protect children from unwanted sexual experiences and at the same time leave them free to determine the content of their own sexual experiences."[146]

NAMBLA was a major contributor to ILGA, the largest global LGBTQ+ network of more than 400 associations worldwide, until it was excluded from it in 1993 after several scandals and arrests. In the 2000s, it emerged that NAMBLA and some of its members were involved in an international paedophilia network.[147]

In 1979, for the Gay March on Washington, a political document was produced which included a proposal for a Gay Youth Caucus calling for "Full rights for gay youth, including revision of the Age of Consent Act."[148] Only one lesbian association threatened not to participate in the march unless this claim was removed.

In the process of the social acceptance of a practice and an idea—from the unthinkable and inconceivable, to the extreme, but possible, to being considered as acceptable and reasonable to its generalisation and legalisation—as far as paedophilia is

---

146 Roy Radow. *NAMBLA Replies to ILGA Secretariat*. 1994. <http://www.qrd.org/qrd/orgs/NAMBLA/nambla.replies.to.ilga.secretariat>, accessed 23 May 2023. Archived on 28 June 2015. In Enrica Perucchietti and Gianluca Marletta. Op.cit. Footnote 140.

147 <https://it.wikipedia.org/wiki/NAMBLA#cite_note-boston-3>; see also Sheila Jeffreys, *Penile Imperialism: The Male Sex Right and Women's Subordination*. Chapter 5: The Paedophile Liberation Movement. Australia, Mission Beach: Spinifex Press. 2022.

148 Full Rights for Gay Youth, including revision of the age of consent laws. <https://it.wikipedia.org/wiki/NAMBLA#cite_note-boston-3>.

concerned, society today is entering the stage of considering it extreme, but possible.

The mainstream press and academia have begun to convey the idea of paedophilia as a *sexual orientation* and to give voice to the testimonies of paedophiles. Here are a few examples by way of illustration.

In 1998, the American Psychiatric Association (APA) issued a report downplaying the traumatic effects of sexual relations between adults and minors[149] and in 2013, the DSM-5 (Diagnostic and Statistical Manual of Mental Disorders) outlined that sexual desire for children is a "sexual orientation."[150] Later, following a "concern that this would pave the way for less criminal culpability," it retracted this statement by clarifying that:

> The American Psychological Association maintains that pedophilia is a mental disorder; that sex between adults and children is always wrong; and that acting on pedophilic impulses is and should be a criminal act. (American Psychological Association, 2013, p. x).

However, other sources agree that a paedophilic disorder is a sexual preference (Harvard University, 2010).[151]

---

[149] <https://www.greeleygazette.com/pres/?p=11517>. Archived on 3 July 2011.

[150] <https://www.ilfoglio.it/articoli/2013/11/05/news/gli-psichiatri-usa-sdoganano-la-pedofilia-da-malattia-a-orientamento-56238/>, accessed 14 February 2022.

[151] David Porter. 'Pedophilic Disorder DSM-5'. 302.2 (F65.4). <https://www.theravive.com/therapedia/pedophilic-disorder-dsm>. 5-302.2-(F65.4), accessed 14 February 2022. <https://www.theravive.com/therapedia/pedophilic-disorder-dsm--5-302.2-(f65.4)>.

In 2014, in Australia, a judge, on delivering a verdict on a man who had abused his sister when he was 17 and she was 11, said that the statement paedophilia and incest would someday be accepted as homosexuality is accepted today.[152]

Also in 2014, a conference was held at Cambridge University in England that established that "paedophilic interest is natural and normal for the human male."[153]

In October 2014, *The New York Times* published the article 'Pedophilia: A Disorder, Not a Crime'.[154] In 2015, the letter/article 'I am a paedophile, but not a monster', was published in *Salon*.[155]

In 2018, at a TED Talk conference in Germany[156] it was argued that paedophilia was not a choice, but an immutable trait of a person.

Allyn Walker's 2022 book, *A Long Dark Shadow: Minor-Attracted People and Their Pursuit of Dignity,* is "a crucial account of the lived experiences of this hidden population"[157] in order to destigmatise adults who are sexually attracted to prepubescent

---

152 <https://www.tempi.it/australia-giudice-sdogana-incesto-e-pedofilia-non-siamo-negli-anni-50-non-siano-piu-tabu-come-omosessualita/>, accessed 14 February 2022.
153 <https://www.telegraph.co.uk/comment/10948796/Paedophilia-is-natural-and-normal-for-males.html>.
154 <https://www.nytimes.com/2014/10/06/opinion/pedophilia-a-disorder-not-a-crime.html>.
155 <https://www.independent.co.uk/news/world/americas/i-m-a-paedophile-not-a-monster-claims-us-man-10512893.html>.
156 <https://www.youtube.com/watch?v=knaxQPjHn2k>.
157 Julie Bindel. 'Call a child rapist a "child rapist"'. In *The Critic*. 2021. <https://thecritic.co.uk/call-a-child-rapist-a-child-rapist/>, accessed 14 February 2022.

children. Paedophiles are thus redefined as 'Minor-Attracted People'. The author casually states that,

> it is important to say 'Minor-Attracted People' out of respect for the terminology that members of that group want others to use for them. It is less stigmatizing than other words like pedophile.[158]

However, I make Julie Bindel's words my own: "Call a child rapist a 'child rapist.'"[159]

In parallel, the process of hypersexualisation of girls conveyed through the media is amplified, with the movie *Cuties* released on Netflix in 2020 being one example.

I have long thought that queer transactivist claims and positions, in their absence of putting limits, in the erasure of the family, in the self-determination of adolescents taken to the extreme, would, sooner or later, make it likely that the idea of a possible legitimisation of paedophilia would emerge—obviously always first claiming 'consent' by girls and boys, and denouncing any abuse or violence. A beginning of this process may be seen in the call for the lowering of the age of sexual consent for minors. Such a request was made in 2021 by ILGA:

> Eliminate all laws and policies that punish or criminalize same-sex intimacy, gender affirmation, abortion, HIV transmission non-disclosure and exposure, or that limit the exercise of bodily autonomy, including laws limiting legal capacity of adolescents.[160]

---

158 Julie Bindel. Op.cit. Footnote 157.
159 Julie Bindel. Op.cit. Footnote 157.
160 Marina Terragni. 'ILGA Il cartello mondiale LGTQ chiede l'abbassamento dell'età del consenso sessuale per le/i minori e chiama abusivamente la sua

Gender Ideology and Paedophilia

Immediate criticism came from the LGB Alliance, an organisation that had exited from the Stonewall cartel:

> This is confusing. The ILGA Declaration signed by Stonewall calls for an end to legal restrictions on adolescent sexual consent. The United Nations and the World Health Organization define adolescence as the age between 10 and 19. If you do not want to find yourself regretting supporting this policy proposal, please clarify.[161]

Once again, the rhetoric of 'freedom of choice' and 'self-determination' is instrumental in glossing over horrors. The same rhetoric has already served to sugarcoat other realities: the buying and selling of baby girls and boys in the practice of 'womb-for-rent' resignified as *gestation for others* (surrogacy); the commodification, exploitation and violence in prostitution resignified as *sex-worker*.

Will gender ideology's next step be to re-signify paedophilia as a new sexual 'orientation'? Indeed, this is already happening.

---

richiesta femminista'. In *Feminist Post*. 14 April 2021. <https://feministpost.it/primo-piano/ilga-cartello-mondiale-lgbtq-chiede-labbassamento-delleta-del-consenso-sessuale-per-le-i-minori-e-chiama-abusivamente-la-sua-richiesta-femminista/>, accessed 14 February 2022.

161 Marina Terragni. Op.cit. Footnote 160.

Chapter 21

Who Funds the LGBTQ+ Movement?[162]

Funding for the LGBTQ+ transactivist movement comes from many foundations and organisations, such as George Soros' Open Society Foundations (OSF), to name the most well-known. Lesser known but particularly significant is the Terasem Movement Foundation of 'transhumanist' Martine Rothblatt, an 'MtF transhumanist' and CEO of United Therapeutics, a multinational pharmaceutical and biotechnology company committed to new biomedical technologies and xenotransplantation, on whose board of directors sits well-known 'transhumanist' Ray Kurzweil. Rothblatt owns the largest company to clone pigs for xenotransplantation in a research project in partnership with

---

[162] Much of the information in this chapter comes from Jennifer Bilek and Paul Cudenec:
Jennifer Bilek. 'Who Are the Rich, White Men Institutionalizing Transgender Ideology?' and Jennifer Bilek. 'The billionaires behind the lgbt movement'. <https://www.firstthings.com/web-exclusives/2020/01/the-billionaires-behind-the-lgbt-movement>. 2020.
Paul Cudenec. 'Controlling the left: the impact edgenda'. <https://winteroak.org.uk/2021/02/10/controlling-the-left-the-impact-edgenda/> and 'Guerrillas of the Great Reset'. <https://winteroak.org.uk/2020/11/20/guerrillas-of-the-great-reset/>. 2021.

Synthetic Genomics, a multinational synthetic biology company owned by well known biotechnologist, Craig Venter.[163]

Rothblatt is also a member of the National Academies of Science, Engineering and Medicine, funded by DARPA (Defense Advanced Research Projects Agency).[164] Rothblatt, like other 'transhumanists' engaged in public dissemination, has written several books for the general public on DNA mapping, genetic screening, artificial reproduction of human beings and transgenderism.

The Terasem Foundation invests in research projects on nano- and biotechnology, cyborg-consciousness, cryogenics and artificial intelligence by promoting 'transhumanist' ideology to the general public. The following is one of its offerings: the BioFile Programme. In this programme, you are invited to store your live cells, with their biological clocks stopped for an indefinite amount of time:

> We collect the live cells from your sample and store them at liquid nitrogen temperature (-90°C) for an indefinite period of time. After you have been declared legally dead, future technology may be able

---

[163] Craig Venter was head of the Human Genome Project and the Minimal Genome Project. The goal of the latter was not only to decode the genome, but to redesign it with synthetic biology. A US Department of Defence government agency is in charge of developing new technologies for military use.

[164] Jennifer Bilek. 'The Gender Identity Industry, Transhumanism and Posthumanism'. September 2022. ≤https://jbilek.substack.com/p/the-gender-identity-industry-transhumanism>.

to grow you a new body via ectogenesis and your mindfile may be able to be downloaded into it, enabling you to live on indefinitely.[165]

Following the project of uploading consciousness into a computer, Rothblatt also developed a robot with the face of his wife, Bina48, to achieve the transcendence longed for by 'transhumanists'.

These and other individuals are not simply among the richest men on the planet, entrepreneurs, executives of multinational biomedical and biotechnology corporations—with the investments of their companies, their philanthropic works, and their research projects they are in a position to direct the world's policy agenda.

We have to wonder where this interest of the universal masters in protecting the rights of a minority of the population comes from.

A statement by a US congressman nicely highlights the interests at stake: "The medical-industrial complex in this country is bigger than the military-industrial complex. And people don't recognize that, but it is a huge industry that is resisting change."[166]

But the complexity of these processes cannot be reduced to new markets and new profits, especially when we consider that financing them are entities that hold capital exceeding the GDP of entire countries—their purpose therefore cannot be merely profit.

---

165 <https://terasemmovementfoundation.com/mission#7>, accessed 6 October 2021.
166 Rep. McDermott. 'The Medical-Industrial Complex in this Country is Bigger than the Military-Industrial Complex'. <https://www.democracynow.org/2009/4/1/rep_mcdermott_the_medical_industrial_complex>.

A brief overview of some of these major funders is helpful in understanding the world from which they come and their close ties to the fields of techno-scientific and transactivist research and development.

These funders often come through anonymous funding organisations such as the Tides Foundation, founded and run by Drummond Pike. Major corporations, philanthropists, and organisations can send huge sums of money to the Tides Foundation, which in turn makes sure it reaches its destination anonymously. The Tides Foundation creates a tax shelter for foundations and also funds political campaigns.

These funders, along with pharmaceutical companies and the US government, are sending millions of dollars to LGBTQ+ causes. Total global spending on LGBTQ+ is currently estimated at US$424 million. From 2003 to 2013, funding has increased more than eightfold.

In the past decade, more than 30 clinics for girls and boys with alleged gender dysphoria have sprung up in the United States alone. The Center for Transyouth Health and Development at the Children's Hospital in Los Angeles is the largest clinic in the country with more than 700 young people in treatment. The youngest is three years old. Over the last ten years, there has also been an explosion of transgender medical infrastructure in the United States and around the world. Interventions range from plastic surgery to uterine transplants for men who identify as women and now may desire their own pregnancies. These surgeries have unfortunately already been tried out on other animals. Biogenetics is poised to be the investment of the future, says Martine Rothblatt, who points to biogenetics and transplantation.

Open Societies Foundation (OSF) in 2011–13 was the lead funder of the transgender cause followed by Stryker's Arcus Foundation and Pritzker's Tawani Foundation.[167]

OSF fully promotes the goals of transgender activists, arguing that biological sex should be replaced by subjective 'gender identity' to include options "outside the binary categories of male and female"; that identity should not be "governed by age limits" and advocates access to "hormone therapy, counselling, and gender affirmation surgeries" upon request including puberty blockers for youth.[168]

OSFs work is not merely an influence, but a definite direction toward affirming 'gender identity'. Significantly, its report published in 2015 was entitled 'License to be Yourself: Trans Children and Youth'[169] within its Public Health Program.

The Pritzkers are an American family of billionaire philanthropists, and their main areas of investment are directed toward the transgender cause, to introduce this ideology into medical and educational institutions with a thread linking these investments

---

167 Jennifer Bilek. Op.cit. Footnote 162.
168 Overview of the 2017 budget of Open Society Foundations: <https://www.opensocietyfoundations.org/sites/default/files/open-society-foundations-2017-budget-overview-20170202.pdf>.
169 Open Society Foundations. 'License to Be Yourself: Trans Children and Youth'. 2015. <https://www.opensocietyfoundations.org/publications/trans-children-and-youth>.

to biomedicine and artificial reproduction. Their most significant investments are: Lurie Children's Hospital, a medical centre for children with presumed gender dysphoria; a chair in transgender studies; the Pritzker School of Medicine at the University of Chicago; the Cleveland Clinic, which conducted the first uterus transplant in the United States; the Baylor College of Medicine where in 2017 the first child was born from a uterus transplant and in-vitro fertilization, as part of their research program to develop uterus transplants. (For this, they took the uterus from each of ten women, transplanted them into ten other women, performed IVF on them and finally delivered the children with a caesarian.)

Then there is the Palm Center, an LGBTQ+ think-tank at the University of California, engaged in research aimed at validating transgenderism in the military; the Clinical Innovations, which is one of the largest medical device companies and in 2017 acquired Brenner Medical for innovative products in the areas of obstetrics and gynaecology; Duke University, engaged in research projects to cryopreserve women's ovaries; and Planned Parenthood, whose clinics now also provide hormone therapy pathways. Planned Parenthood consists of several national organisations that are members of the International Planned Parenthood Federation (IPPF), which is headed by clinics where abortions are performed that have been at the centre of scandals related to the harvesting, use and trade of tissues and organs used for medical research and from aborted foetuses and partial-birth abortions at 20 weeks of pregnancy.[170]

The Planned Parenthood Federation of America along with the Human Rights Campaign (HRC) Foundation launched a campaign to reshape cultural narratives of sexuality and reproductive health based on artificial reproduction of the human.

A member of the Pritzker family served as Secretary of Commerce during the Obama presidency, helping to create the National Institute for Innovation in Manufacturing Biopharmaceuticals which is engaged in vaccines, gene therapies, microchips and currently in research projects to run the new pandemic-friendly techno-medical society.

'Arcus Foundation Push Boundaries', the slogan with which the Arcus Foundation (AF) presents itself, is a charity and the world's largest LGBTQ+ non-governmental organisation, founded by Jon Stryker, heir to a medical technology company.

Stryker has built a political infrastructure to drive the ideology of 'gender identity' around the world, donating millions to entities large and small. To ILGA, an LGBT equality organisation in Europe and Central Asia with 54 participating countries along with Transgender Europe, this foundation has donated hundreds of thousands of dollars. To Stonewall, the largest LGBTQ

---

[170] 'Undercover video shows Planned Parenthood official discussing fetal organs used for research. *Washington Post*. 2015. <https://www.washingtonpost.com/politics/undercover-video-shows-planned-parenthood-exec-discussing-organ-harvesting/2015/07/14/ae330e34-2a4d-11e5-bd33-395c05608059_story.html>, accessed 9 July 2021.

association in Europe, this foundation has donated $142,000 just before it added the T to LGB and expanded its mandate to cover transgender issues. The thread that binds the Arcus Foundation to Stonewall is a thread woven of funding including $75,000 to finance Stonewall to participate in roundtables to convince business to support the LGBTQ+ cause by portraying it as "a good business strategy."[171]

Among the many projects funded by Arcus is Rainbow Laces, a project aimed at bringing LGBTQ+ people into sport, thus opening women's sports to 'trans MtF' people.

President Biden, formerly Obama's vice president, follows the path that has already been well-trodden. In 2021, he approved a bill in which 'gender identity' took precedence over women's rights based on sex.[172] In 2022, he advanced the 'transhumanist' agenda by signing an Executive Order on the Advancement of Innovation in Biotechnology, which called for the development of genetic engineering techniques,

> to be able to write circuits for cells and predictably program biology in the same way we write software and program computers, as well

---

[171] Jennifer Bilek. 'Big Pharma Exploits and Monetizes "Trans Identity"'. In *The 11th Hour*. <https://www.the11thhourblog.com/post/big-pharma-exploits-and-monetizes-trans-identity>, accessed 24 October 2021.

[172] Reagan McCarthy 'President Biden Signs Executive Order Prioritizing "Gender Identity" Over Biology', in *Townhall*, 21 January 2021. <https://townhall.com/tipsheet/reaganmccarthy/2021/01/21/biden-eo-title-ix-n2583491>, accessed 26 April 2023.

as genetic technologies to 'unlock the power of biological data' using 'computer tools and artificial intelligence'.[173]

Biden, in 2023, with the modification of a law on discrimination based on sex, required the access of men who identify as women to women's sports. A political struggle ensued that has not concluded.

There have been strong protests from sportswomen who see themselves crushed by physical differences in sports performance by so-called transwomen (men). In March 2023, the World Athletics Federation (World Athletics) established that biologically male 'trans' people will not be able to compete in international women's competitions. Similar bans have also been introduced by the International Rugby League and the International Swimming Federation. But the inclusion of transgender people in women's sports (or not) remains an open chapter.

It should be noted that for FtMs there are no specific projects; 'trans FtM' people are only instrumentally used when they become pregnant after testosterone interruption, but in fact, this only highlights that everyone is born from a woman, a reality that cannot be denied.

Arcus has also provided funding of $650,000 to the leading psychology organisation in the US, the American Psychological

---

[173] Dr Joseph Mercola, 'The Transhumanist Agenda Behind Biden's Executive Order on 'Advancing Biotechnology'. 26 September 2022 in *Children's Health Defender*. <https://childrenshealthdefense.org/defender/transhumanist-agenda-biden-executive-order-biotechnology-cola/>, accessed 26 April 2023.

Association (APA), which develops guidelines for establishing trans-affirmative psychological treatment paths.

In 2001, with the help of funding from Arcus, the APA established INET (International Psychology Network for LGBTIQ, later called IpsyNet) and, in 2005, created the Task Force on Gender Identity and Gender Variance.

With the birth of IpsyNet, psychologists were encouraged to "modify their understanding of 'gender' by expanding the range of variations seen as healthy and normative."[174] The Task Force's report on 'gender identity' states that sex "refers to attributes that characterize biological maleness and femaleness" (p. 28). The report decouples 'gender' from sex, stating that 'gender' is a "basic sense of being male, female, or of indeterminate sex" (p. 28).

This confuses sex with 'gender'. How does one 'feel' like the female or male sex, or neither? People are simply male or female. One can't know what an oppositely sexed body feels any more than one can know what it feels like to be a dolphin.

In Child Trends, a leading research organisation interested in the lives of children and young people, we find that significant funding came from Arcus to carry out a study in 2017 called 'Improving measurement of sexual orientation and 'gender identity' among middle and high school students'. From the

---

174 Jennifer Bilek. 'Capturing the American Psychological Association: The Engineering of Human Sexual Evolution'. In *The 11th Hour*. <https://www.the11thhourblog.com/post/capturing-the-american-psychological-association-the-engineering-of-human-sexual-evolution>, accessed 25 October 2021.

pages of this study emerges the idea that children can be born in the body of the wrong sex.

Media narratives are also subject to skilful manipulation. Organisations involved in journalism or film-documentary production receive funding from Arcus. The aim is to ensure that media coverage is shaped by the Trans Lobby.

At a 2008 meeting in Bellagio, Italy, at the headquarters of the Rockefeller Foundation, 29 international leaders pledged to expand global philanthropy to support LGBTQ+ rights. Outside the Bellagio meeting, the Arcus Foundation created the Movement Advancement Project, a project to advance the LGBTQ+ movement, to chart the complex system of advocacy and funding that would promote 'gender identity/transgenderism' in the wider culture.[175]

In 2013, Adrian Coman—a veteran of George Soros' Open Society Foundation—was appointed director of the international human rights programme at the Arcus Foundation, to drive the ideology of 'gender identity' globally.

There is also no shortage of speculative investment funds, such as the Edge Funds, investing in London Trans+ Pride. The Rockefeller Foundation co-chaired Edge's programme committee and on the board of Edge Funders, we find a representative of the Open Society Initiative for Europe.

---

[175] Jennifer Bilek. 'Who Are the Rich, White Men Institutionalizing Transgender Ideology?' and Jennifer Bilek. 'The billionaires behind the lgbt movement'. 2020. <https://www.firstthings.com/web-exclusives/2020/01/the-billionaires-behind-the-lgbt-movement>.

And of course, there is BlackRock, whose CEO Larry Fink is co-chair of the trustees of NYU Langone Health, which runs the Transgender Youth Health Program that offers support for "medical interventions for gender affirmation, including puberty suppression, hormone treatments for gender affirmation, and gender affirmation surgery."[176] BlackRock also owns 4.7% of the shares of AbbVie, the manufacturer of the puberty-blocking drug Lupron.

Vanguard is the largest shareholder of Marqeta Inc., a global credit card issuance platform. Visa, with Marqeta Inc., supports Daylight, the new 'queer credit card' and digital banking platform. Daylight markets its card to sell assisted reproduction and surrogacy services to the lesbian and gay community and to those adolescents who will be pushed towards the transition path,[177] considering that, once rendered sterile by blockers and hormones, if they want to have children, they will be able to do so only through artificial reproduction clinics.

Funding also comes from pharmaceutical multinationals and their foundations, such as Pfizer and Johnson and Johnson's Janssen Therapeutics Foundation, and from big data multinationals such as Google, Microsoft, Amazon, Intel and IBM.

---

176 Alan Neale. 'Why would the world's largest fund management corporation support a UK charity for LGBT Youth?' In *The 11th Hour*. 2021. <https://www.the11thhourblog.com/post/why-would-the-world-s-largest-fund-management-corporation-support-a-small-uk-charity-for-lgbt-youth>, accessed 24 October 2021.

177 Jennifer Bilek. 'Humanity for Sale'. In *American Mind*. <https://americanmind.org/features/soul-dysphoria/humanity-for-sale/ >, accessed 24 April 2023.

In the political world, I draw attention to Petra de Sutter, a transsexual MtF Belgian politician of the Green Party, and since October 2020 a deputy prime minister and first transgender minister in Europe. He is at the forefront of driving the technological colonisation of female reproductive capabilities, the 'gender identity' industry, and CRISPR technology.

In addition to his role in the Senate, in 2016 he was assembly speaker on children's rights in relation to surrogacy agreements and, in 2017, on the use of new genetic technologies applied to human beings. He popularises the potential of genetic editing in artificial reproduction—without women—and transhumanist ideology.

Some of the funding for the LGBTQ+ cause is aimed at creating grassroots movements, and as Susan Hawthorne has stated:

> Astroturfing is a very 21st-century means of advocacy. Organisations mask their sources of funding to give the appearance of being a grassroots organisation. Just as astroturf is fake grass, astroturfing refers to organisations that are fake grassroots, i.e. a phoney movement. Astroturfing is especially prominent in the US, but has spread around the world and is prominent among transgender and 'sex work' advocates.[178]

Jennifer Bilek has delved into the funders of the transgender movement and has argued that when millions of dollars are

---

[178] "Just as the transgender organisations are well-funded, so too are prostitution rings." In Susan Hawthorne. 2020. *Vortex: The Crisis of Patriarchy*, Mission Beach: Spinifex Press. p. 80 and p. 134.

invested to develop a movement, it is artificial weed. It will not be a real grassroots movement, but a project of the elite.

Many of us are trying to point this out to radical left groups that scream "trans women are women" and especially to leftist feminists: you are being manipulated by billionaires. This is not a grassroots movement, it is an elite project, a lot of money is being invested to promote a dissociative body condition that unties us from our sexed bodies.

The LGBTQ+ cause is now high on the agenda of the powerful, and its advocates are at the top of the media, in academia, and especially in Big Business, Big Philanthropy, and Big Tech.

Chapter 22

From the Laboratory to Queer Cyborg Activism

Nature does not exist, we are told:

> *In a world where progressives have denied nature*, progress consists in seeing ourselves as progressive because we sell children bought from poor women who put their wombs up for rent; […] it consists in consuming products made by an industrial complex that privileges […] genetic modification; it consists in intoxicating oneself even by simply breathing, drinking water or seeking medical care; it consists in turning sexuality into one of the modes of commerce and consumerism; it consists in turning a sexual relationship into a virtual relationship; […] it consists in making it so that assisted procreation can also allow 'men' to get pregnant, for equality issues; it consists in demanding from the civil registrar that one can change one's age because one feels less old.[179]

Queer and trans cyborg-faux-feminism does not need nature because in its premises it has already replaced nature with synthetic biology.

---

179 Michel Onfray. Op.cit. Footnote 2.

Martine Rothblatt asserts that we are all *transhumans*, that changing our bodies by removing healthy tissues and organs and ingesting cross-sex hormones over the course of a lifetime can be likened to putting on make-up, dyeing our hair, or getting a tattoo. This means normalising the alteration of human biology, the genetic modification of bodies. In his book, *From Transgender to Transhuman*, Rothblatt states, "Ensuring the ethical use of biotechnology will be as large a concern for transhumanists as it is for defenders of gender freedom."[180]

Rothblatt, in 2016, during the Trans History Forward Movement conference organised by the Canadian University of Victoria's Transgender Chair, stated that techno-transhumanists attempt to use the same procedures as techno-transgenders to make legal changes that allow alterations in human biology. In his 2008 journal article, 'Are We Transbemans Yet?' he writes about re-conceptualising the species boundary and posits bio-nanotechnology, generative biology, and artificial intelligence as cornerstones of the new transman [sic].[181]

So-called 'transhumanists'. George Dvorsky and James Hughes wrote in 2008:

> Our contemporary efforts at creating gender-neutral societies have also reached the limits of biological gender. Today, however, biotechnologies, neurotechnologies and information technologies

---

180 Martine Rothblatt. *From Transgender to Transhuman: A Manifesto on the Freedom of Form.* Self-published. 2011.
181 Martine Rothblatt. 'Are we Transbemans Yet?' In *Journal of Evolution and Technology*, Vol. 18, Issue 1. May 2008, pp. 94–107. <http://jetpress.org/v18/rothblatt.htm>.

make it possible to complete the project of freeing ourselves from patriarchy and the constraints of binary gender. Postgender technologies will put an end to static biological and sexual self-identification, allowing individuals to decide for themselves which biological and psychological gender traits they wish to keep or reject.[182]

Radical feminists were already warning years ago about this, about how transactivist cyborg queer ideologies run together with instances of this techno-scientific and trans(faux)humanist system and how wanting to erase all boundaries and, in fact, erase the material reality of bodies, represents a meeting point between transactivist, queer and 'transhumanist' ideologies.

But despite all the works of deconstruction, we *are* human beings, not hybrids, monsters or cyborgs, and we *are* all born from women, from mothers.

Next I discuss what Donna Haraway wonders about a multitude and large family of fellow species: aliens, hybrids, surrogates, living instruments, oncomice, queer, cyborgs and, as the latest arrivals, multispecies humus and children of compost. In Haraway's words: "How, in the context of the current cultural situation, could feminists and anti-racists dispense with the power of the laboratory to put in doubt what is deemed normal?"[183]

The cyborg, for its supporters, is a creature in a post-gender world not generated by biological sexual procreation. It is a

---

182 George Dvorsky and James Hughes. *Postgenderism: Beyond the Gender Binary*. Boston: PhD Institute for Ethics and Emerging Technologies. 2008.
183 Donna J. Haraway. *Testimone-modesta@femaleman-incontra-Oncotopo: Femminismo e tecnoscienza*. Milano: Feltrinelli. 2000.

figure subversive of the system, a figure that challenges the sexual differences between female and male, the differences between nature and artefact, between human and machine. These differences have been deleted. The cyborg is a fusion between organic and inorganic, between flesh and silicon where the boundaries of the body no longer coincide with the skin. Technology pervades the body, which becomes the object of technological intervention. Indeed, these technological transformations and fusions would be unimaginable and impossible without the developments of the techno-sciences.

The vision of the body as a machine, as an image of the 'multiple and denaturalised subject' is defended by many including Haraway and Rothblatt. The artefact, the simulacrum, the genetically modified organism, the virtual dimension that becomes a new habitat produces the new parameters of the new subjectivity. Subjectivity is rethought in relation to the techno-sciences, which become the main tools for dismantling, redesigning and reconstructing bodies. In these postmodern drifts, the body is "an invention," "a malleable and moldable entity," "a techno-modifiable entity," "a technology to be hacked," "a reworkable platform in which biotechnology can offer new possibilities."[184]

As that most progressive fan of all transhumans, Yuval Noah Harari — adviser to Klaus Schwab, President of the Word Economic Forum (WEF) — reminds us how to describe

---

184 Carlotta Cossutta, Valentina Greco, Arianna Mainardi and Stefania Voli. *Smagliature digitali, corpi, generi e tecnologie*. Milan: Agenzia X. 2018.

'the equation of life' in the 21st century: knowledge of biology combined with computing power and the acquisition of data can lead to the ability to "hack the human being. If you know enough biology and have enough computing power you can hack my body, my brain and my very life."[185]

Once again these are moments of encounter where 'trans'-feminism and transhumanism have the same aspirations.

Transforming the body into a platform has always been present in transhumanist projects. Today we need only to read their programmes, such as the report 'Human Augmentation — The Dawn of a New Paradigm, a Strategic Implications Project'[186] on the scientific objectives of the Ministries of Defence in the UK and Germany which basically mirror those of the US Department of Defence, the WEF and other transhumanist elites. On page 12 of the report, the concept of the human body as a platform is described and among the technologies for "being able to augment the various parts of the human platform," we find genetics, germline modification, synthetic biology, external and internal brain interfaces.

Genetic manipulation and genetic mutations caused by toxicity hark back to the manipulation of bodies and that underlying but ever-present obsession with nature. They hark back

---

185 <https://www.youtube.com/watch?v=Gjlskk07ES0>, accessed 26 April 2023.
186 Ministry of Defence. 'Human Augmentation — The Dawn of a New Paradigm, a Strategic Implications Project'. May 2021. <chrome-extension://efaidnbmnnnibpcajpcglclefindmkaj/https://assets.publishing.service.gov.uk/government/uploads/system/uploads/attachment_data/file/986301/Human_Augmentation_SIP_access2.pdf>.

to the aversion to carnality, finitude, the contingencies and uncertainties of life. Genetic mutations represent "ambiguity, variability, mutability."[187] The effects of endocrine disruptors such as benzene, dioxin, PCBs ... would fall within "a malleable ontology of life": a "toxic queerness."[188] It is no coincidence that "biotechnologies for trans body mutation"[189] and artificial reproduction technologies are placed at the centre.

Queer transactivist theorists ask, why not invest in the dissemination of hormone therapies to get men to breastfeed, grant access to IVF techniques for the LGBTQ+ movement, and advocate genetic engineering, cloning, ectogenesis and gene editing including with CRISPR/Cas 9?[190] Behind their obsessive demands for having access to MAPs, one cannot assume that there is simply a desire for a child, as these demands are often brought forward by those who have an obvious aversion to motherhood and children.[191]

Artificial reproduction of human beings viewed as freedom and emancipation brings us back to the thoughts of Shulamith Firestone who, in the early 1970s, considered the artificial womb a possibility to free women from the 'biological tyranny' and 'barbarity' of pregnancy. Over time, this has generated a disincarnation with one's sexed body, and a split between the woman and the possibility for procreation—which belongs to the

---

187 Helen Hester. *Xenofeminism*. Cambridge and Oxford: Polity Books. 2018.
188 Helen Hester. Op.cit. Footnote 187.
189 Cossutta *et al*. Op.cit. Footnote 184.
190 Angela Balzano. *Per farla finita con la famiglia*. Rome: Meltemi. 2021.
191 Angela Balzano. Op.cit. Footnote 190.

woman regardless of whether or not she gives birth to a child—a dimension that has been appropriated by the medical and techno-scientific system and by the fertility market to medicalise it, pathologise it, fragment it, artificialise it. This is done by dissolving the central role of the mother-daughter relationship, the carnal and symbolic foundation of every community.

Today all of this has produced a paradox: basically 'trans'feminism despises procreation and birth, but forcefully claims it through surrogacy and the prospect of artificial wombs for infertile and LGBTQ+ people.

The movement in this direction is a desire to break every boundary, and a fascination with techno-science and body modification that can only reaffirm the laboratory paradigm from which it was produced.

A hybrid, that is, an infertile being, acquires a positive and subversive meaning by erasing the reality of what it is: a transgenic animal for research. And genetic chimeras no longer go back to the laboratory that produced them. Do people realise that the much quoted oncomouse is a female mouse that was inoculated with cancer in DuPont laboratories?[192]

Anything that comes out of a laboratory cannot be considered as potentially disrupting the power structure with which it is imbued, at least unless one considers scientific research itself to be neutral. However, techno-sciences are not neutral, not only

---

[192] Douglas Hanahan, Erwin F. Wagner, Richard D. Palmiter. 'The origins of oncomice: a history of the first transgenic mice genetically engineered to develop cancer'. *Genes Dev.* 2007. <https://pubmed.ncbi.nlm.nih.gov/17875663/>.

in what they set out to achieve—whether they actually do so or not—but already upstream, in their ideas of redesigning the world that makes bodies available, 'dismemberable' and modifiable.

In *Staying with Trouble: Making Kin in the Chthulucene*,[193] Donna J. Haraway has written a book that is much praised and regarded as a denunciation of anthropocentrism and capitalist exploitation of the Earth, but which in reality is something quite different.[194] It follows the same path as the Green Economy and the Great Reset. The chapter 'The Children of Compost' describes an imaginary world ruled by scientists in which all boys and girls will have three parents, are born through artificial reproduction, are genetically modified with genes from other species, are born without a sex, and in the course of their lives, can further modify their own bodies.

Unfortunately, these are not just the flights of fancy of those who from academic offices can afford to philosophise: their catchy rhetoric penetrates powerfully, and shapes and re-shapes all those writings that once expressed a critique of capitalism and its exploitations. This rhetoric does not remain mere abstract speculation, but morphs into political claims and ideologies that reinforce this techno-scientific system within which they are fully located.

---

[193] Donna J. Haraway. *Staying with Trouble. Making Kin in the Chthulucene.* Durham and London: Duke University Press. 2016.
[194] By using the word 'chthulu', Donna Haraway is suggesting that she is echoing earth-dwelling creatures—from the Greek word 'chthonic'. But this is a misrepresentation, since the realm of the chthonic was one in which female figures prevailed.

In the new glitter rainbow paradigm, the word 'cisgender' becomes the norm and the word 'woman' becomes reactionary. "MtF people freeze the stereotypes of fabulous femininity and exalt them. They thus do the exact opposite of what feminists want to do, which is to destroy gender."[195]

As summed up by the lesbian feminist group from Milan:

> The transgender movement is neither progressive nor radical because it has no wish to transcend the limitations of capitalism but rather to isolate the signifiers of a socially constructed femininity in order to reinforce and reproduce them. Therefore, the potential for a radical rejection of a patriarchal capitalist society is impossible within trans ideology, which works to maintain the divisions that contribute to its continuing existence. […] The rise of individualism and the centring of the individual wants human rights at the expense of collective needs. [They] represent both the extension of a consumer society and the guarantee of its reproduction. It means nothing is safe if anything can be appropriated, if anything can be claimed to belong to those who simply want it or feel it, without situating that want within the social relations within which it is embedded.[196]

In all of this, political discourse and action become mired and are reduced to a mere victimised and whining claim that closes

---

[195] Deidre O'Neill. 'Left censorship and exclusion against gender-critical women: a Marxist critique'. 2019. <https://rdln.wordpress.com/2019/11/17/left-censorship-and-exclusion-against-gender-critical-women-a-marxist-critique/>.

[196] Cristina Gramolini, Sabina Zenobi, Flavia Franceschini, Lucia Giansiracusa and Stella Zaltieri Pirola *Noi, le lesbiche. Preferenza al femminile e critica al transfemminismo*. Milan: Il dito e La luna. 2021.

in on one's individual needs and desires. It is a kaleidoscopic fragmentation of political action into the myriad rivulets of an activism whose field of action does not go beyond claiming a libertarian right for one's own desire. A mere autobiography of the self. But basing needs on the infinite multiplicity of desires and the total commodification of the *desiring machines that we are*—to follow the thinking of Gilles Deleuze, Félix Guattari & company—transforms bodies into *docile bodies*: perfect for the biomarket and a transhumanist society.

Despite what Paul B. Preciado[197] says, taking testosterone is not a political act and does not make one a dissident in a revolution. If we take off the tinsel, we are left with a voluntary intoxication that in fact legitimises and prepares the body to be an arena for experimentation. Preciado, in the course of a lecture in 2019 before an audience of psychoanalysts in which he claimed the need for "trans fatherhood, MAP, surrogacy [and] externalization of the womb,"[198] stated that:

> Making a gender transition means inventing a mechanical adjustment with the hormone or with another living code—the code can be a language, music, a form, a plant, an animal or another living being. [...] This awakening is a revolution. It is a molecular uprising.[199]

---

[197] Paul B. Preciado. *Testo Tossico. Sesso, droghe e biopolitiche nell'era farmacopornografica*. Rome: Fandango Libri. 2015.

[198] Paul B. Preciado. *Sono un mostro che vi parla*. Rome: Fandango Libri. 2021.

[199] Paul B. Preciado. Op.cit. Footnote 198.

This vision becomes ever clearer and moves without any memory of the uprising bodies to divert us directly into the molecular laboratory.

When the horizon of these claims broadens toward social transformation and pseudo-subversion, these desires are wedded to a "capitalism of desire coupled with technology […] that feeds on a fanatical and naive conformism of emancipatory, 'revolutionary' virtues of transgression and infinite limitlessness."[200]

One's subjective desires become objective realities. An infinite multiplicity and recombination of identities, surgical cuts and pharmaceutical intoxications to manufacture fake women and fake men for the interests and ends of the trans industry. And all claimed as freedom and subversion. But the freedom brought about by LBGTQ+ 'trans'feminist claims kills all freedom and there is no subversion of this system, but only an enthusiastic adhesion that promotes their whole agenda.

Freedom is today an abused, tortured and fetishised word. Let us ask ourselves what conception of today's freedom underlies integrity, relationships, feelings, motherhood, body, sexual difference and, ultimately, being human? It is the freedom of atomised and de-sacralised human beings: self-entrepreneurs, without ties, without memory, without roots. It is the freedom of these times of de-sacralisation of the living made not only available, but also consumable.

---

200 Pièces et main d'œuvre. 'Ceci n'est pas une femme (à propos des tordus queer)'. 2014. <https://www.piecesetmaindoeuvre.com/IMG/pdf/Ceci_n_est_pas_une_femme.pdf>.

For these issues, the discussion cannot be about 'freedom of choice'. First of all, freedom of choice is always a rhetorical discourse, always set within the possibilities that a particular system dictates. Freedom is imprisoned in the single horizon of sense and significance that produces the same system. What is represented as the apotheosis of 'free choice' is actually its most radical *negation*, since the individual is subject to a 'choice' that is imposed or induced or made to be desired from the outside.

But even assuming that a choice can be made freely and with awareness, the consequences that go beyond the strictly personal level, extending to *all* bodies and to society as a whole, must not be ignored. The very existence of certain techno-scientific practices and developments admits the possibility of being able to access bodies, opens up the idea that this is ethically acceptable.

Buying and selling of gametes and of boys and girls, mutilations of bodies, hormone bombardments are claimed as rights. But there can be no right to access another body, to fragment and artificialise the dimension of procreation, to have a child at all costs, to destroy children and adolescents.

The dissociation from one's body, its denial, its destruction for an illusion of freedom leads to the loss of the very meaning of freedom, body, human being. Queer 'trans'feminism perfectly embodies today's times characterised by post-truth, denial of values, atomisation. If this context had not existed, the concept of 'gender identity' would not have found a terrain on which to take root and branch out. A terrain that has been prepared for some time, by transnational power oligarchies and specific ideologies.

Chapter 23

The New Transhumanism and Posthuman Humanity

Transhumanist ideology, which is embodied in the projects and aims of Silicon Valley, major research hubs, various foundations and international groups, seeks to dispose of living processes and bodies. Formerly a mere reservoir of raw material, 'transhumanism' aka transactivism seeks to now re-signify them, neutralise them and penetrate inside them, thus irrevocably transforming them. The end goal is to transform the human being and everything living into the artificial, cybernetic and engineered world that will then be redefined and thereby perceived as 'natural' and as the only possible and imaginable world. The goal of 'transhumanism'—transeugenicism by another name—moves ever onward, an imagery that leads an existing human being to conceive of her/himself as an eternally incomplete organism.

In this process, the embryo will be selected, genetically modified and *optimised*. Bodies are no longer just living laboratories in which to experiment with new technologies. Embryos and bodies become platforms into which genetic engineering and cellular redesign technologies, such as recombinant DNA and mRNA can be inserted. They become objects into which human enhancement technologies, such as implantable neural interfaces, and biomedical control technologies such as microchips under the skin will be grafted. Bodies will become 'bodies/communicating platforms': this will be the shift from the Internet of Things to the Internet of Bodies, made possible by the 5G and 6G networks.

Recently, Neuralink—Elon Musk's neurotechnology company—has been given permission to install microchips in Parkinson's patients and in people with prosthetics. As Musk says, "Neuralink's long-term vision is to create BMIs (brain-machine-interfaces) that are sufficiently safe and powerful so that healthy individuals would want to install them."[201] But this post-human will not yet be the perfect human being dreamed of by so-called transhumanists; it will still be a biomedicalised human being from birth to death in an endless self-optimisation and self-implementation.

This is bionanotechnology, artificial intelligence and genetic editing for a global *reset*. The post-human trilogy comes to completion in the convergence of physical, biological and digital transformation.

In all this, 'transhumanist' and eugenicist technocrats need to erase from childhood the biological sex of birth, making way for a 'neutral' humanity, no longer sexed, with no difference between man and woman. The 'neutral' body and body modification paves the way for the construction of the post-human cyborg and the genetic engineering of bodies.

To close the circle of the management and manipulation of the living, they need to appropriate the dimension of procreation

---

201 Elon Musk. <https://neuralink.com/>.

and birth. The erasure of the mother, artificial reproduction technologies, the extension of MAPs, embryo selection and modification, and the artificial womb are milestones along the path to build a post-human and post-nature world.

In the introduction to Jennifer Bilek's blog *The Eleventh Hour* I read these insightful words of hers:

> I write at the intersection of humanity, technology and runaway capitalism. At this intersection stands transgenderism, what I believe is a glamorous ad campaign generated by elites, invested in tech and pharma, to normalize the changing of human biology. I believe this because I have researched the money behind the rapidly growing juggernaut of transgenderism in American culture and beyond, and it all leads back to the pharmaceutical and tech giants that now interface with LGBT NGOs, which are driving the normalization of a biology-denying ideology. This ideology has taken the bullet train of postmodernism to the juncture we are at now. The LGB civil rights movement has been subsumed by elites who have added the T to normalize the overriding of our sexed reality as humans, staging a political coup of mammoth proportion.

'Gender' is an obfuscation. It is the deconstruction of our humanity in its sexed roots that is at issue.

Once we open the door to accepting vast changes to human biology, that undermine the very definition of what it means to be human as a sexually dimorphic species, we have opened up a Pandora's box for melding humans with technology and AI. Transgenderism is, as the famous self-identifying-transgendered, so called 'transhumanist', Martine Rothblatt posits, 'the onramp to the transcendence of fleshism'. As Rothblatt puts it: "people who refuse to be labeled as male or female are the pioneers of seeing humanity as not being limited by any particular substrate, such as flesh. There is a queer line of development from transgender to transhuman."

We have reached the eleventh hour. We have to decide whether we will let go of our humanity in exchange for an elusive and illusory idea of a techno-utopia in which we are told we will never die and can cure, have and be anything we desire thanks to technology.

Or, will we cling to what is left of our humanity while technophilic elites with interests in pharmaceuticals, technology, artificial intelligence, gene splicing, organ transplants and genetic modification that take us far beyond the scope of being human, fight to extract it through a process of capital-driven colonization. [...]

Will we stand on the side of biological reality or will we give way to the technological elites, wedded to the power of profit at the expense of all life, who are leading us over a precipice like the Pied Piper in the children's story?

[...] In genetic and social engineering laboratories there is no room for ethics, but only for the construction and redesign of a post-human humanity. The transhuman rejection of the limit is the rejection of nature, of its borders and, ultimately, it is the rejection of humanity. A humanity without limits and without responsibility is a humanity without humanity.[202]

In November 2018 at the International Summit on Human Genome Editing, a Chinese research group from the Southern University of Science and Technology in Shenzhen announced

---

[202] Jennifer Bilek. *The 11th Hour Blog.* <https://www.the11thhourblog.com/about>.

the birth of two girls genetically modified with CRISPR/Cas9 technology, news that everyone in scientific circles expected and craved—although the researcher, He Jiankui, was condemned for what he had done. This year, in March 2023, in the third edition of *The Summit*, Osaka University presented the results of the research that led to the development of offspring from a pair of male mice using the in vitro gametogenesis (IVG) technique, a technique with which embryos are developed by reprogramming cells taken from two adults of the same sex. This research project follows a previous one from 2018, which had led to the development of offspring starting with pairs of female mice.

It is significant to note that in the debates on the fertility biomarket and the genomic research sector[203] the result of this latest research is promoted as potentially useful for making LGBTQ+ pregnancies feasible because it could, for example, constitute a method used by male couples to have a genetically engineered child related to both men.

These minorities, around which a feeling of pity is created, are and will be used as leverage for the first step, for an extension, to 'create the idea' of a possible realisation of an opportunity provided by a techno-scientific development, as in this case in the field of human reproduction. Thus, the process is originated which sees the beginning of the internalisation of overcoming a further technical and at the same time *ethical* threshold: the

---

[203] Marcin Smietana. 'LGBTQ+ parenthood through in vitro gametogenesis?' 27 March 2023. In *Bionews*. <https://www.progress.org.uk/newsletter_issue/bionews-1184/>, accessed 26 April 2023.

passage through what, being technically possible, becomes ethically acceptable. For everything related to techno-scientific developments and the creation of social acceptance we have the famous Overton window: an idea, a passage, a techno-scientific development initially considered inconceivable, then becomes extreme, then acceptable, then reasonable, up to becoming normal and being generalised.

In the face of everything to which society is not yet accustomed, our voices of indignation must be raised. Let us think of the developments to create an artificial uterus,[204] of the case of the 68-year-old Spanish actress who commissioned a child via surrogate motherhood using her son's cryopreserved sperm before he died from cancer,[205] of the proposal for a "gestational donation of the whole body" in order to use the bodies of 'brain dead' women as containers to continue carrying a pregnancy (and also the bodies of men adapting them for the occasion).[206] And the same people also forcefully demand surrogacy and medically assisted procreation (MAP) for all.

Everyone is scandalised by these monstrosities, but at the same time many people support and promote these techno-

---

204 Silvia Guerini. Un monde sans mères? In 'Les enfants de la Machine. Biotechnologies, reproduction et eugénisme'. *Écologie & Politique*. No. 65, 2022.

205 Jennifer Lahl. 'The lifestyles of the rich and famous'. 11 April 2023. *CBC Network*. <https://cbc-network.org/2023/04/the-lifestyles-of-the-rich-and-famous />, accessed 26 April 2023.

206 Anna Smajdor. 'Whole body gestational donation'. <https://philpapers.org/rec/SMAWBG >, accessed 26 April 2023; Rosalia Ber, 'Ethical Issues in Gestational Surrogacy'. April 2022. <https://link.springer.com/article/10.1023/A:1009956218800>, accessed 26 April 2023.

scientific activities. Furthermore, dwelling only on the aspects that most people would find difficult to support, works to then promote, accelerate and regulate other processes which will eventually still lead to those same extremes that are now greeted with indignation. It is easy to forget that for us to curb this race, it is necessary to take a critical stance *towards all these techno-scientific processes* and to *understand* what is at their root. Is it ethically permissible to want to 'produce' life in the laboratory? Artificialise the procreation process? Engineer the living? Because this is the aim, at every point of the development scale of artificial reproduction techniques.

Other processes, less apparently extreme in people's imagination, are silently running fast. Internationally, there is a push for global governance of CRISPR/Cas 9 for germline genetic modification. We already know the alleged reasons: to avoid the onset of serious genetic diseases. Exactly the same reasons for earlier supporting pre-implantation diagnosis used in the in-vitro fertilisation process, a technique which in itself can produce anomalies in the embryo. And we know, too, the outcome of this process: from the exception for the very serious cases, to the serious ones, then to those considered probable, up to claiming this possibility for all to better optimise the procreation process. From the right to have a child, to the right to have a healthy child, to the right to have a child with genetic improvements. It will not be possible to oppose all of this, as it will be considered a 'right', if the very concept according to which having a child is a right is not fundamentally rejected. We must expect dark times in which infertility and possible genetic alterations will increase. And then, it will be even more difficult to raise any criticism, which will inevitably be considered insane.

From the embryo as product, from 'surrogate motherhood', from the artificial womb, emerges the link with the conception of a fetish body reduced to the state of simple matter to be redesigned. A 'body-thing', a 'body-surrogate', a 'body-platform' in which 'gender identity' is innate and gender 'assigned at birth' is fluid. For the new culture of 'trans-identity' it is the new right to choose one's gender and to mould boys and girls into believing that sex does not exist. A body transformed into a permanent construction site in the 'transition-biomarket' with its biodesign clinics and technomedical bricolage, with its hormones marketed by pharmaceutical multinationals. The infinite proliferation of genres in an infinite modification of techno-bodies and a techno-life engineered and redesigned in the laboratory.

Even the last bioethical barrier is about to be yielded to so-called 'transhumanist' demands, and multiple foundations have already been established to enable a 'neutral' and limitlessly modifiable humanity. *Fluidity* is the antithesis of density, of that which persists, which does not change, which endures and provides a foothold in the earth. The human being, conceived like any fluid, is supposed to be able to take on any form someone may want it to take.

It is urgent to understand these mutations and mystifications of reality where *fluidity* and *deconstruction of meaning* are presented to us as 'progressive': it is precisely their *fluid state* that allows them to be the necessary link between the forces of the pulverisation of the living for the transition to a post-human and post-nature world.

We are witnessing an attack on life. Sex is a bond with life, we are born with a sex, so it is essential to cancel this bond, our first recognition of the world. The new generations are confused, made fragile and unfit for existence in the real world.

We are witnessing an attack on nature, on all that is born. Natural is that what is born, as opposed to artificial, that which is manufactured and "the goal of transhumanism is precisely to replace the natural with the planned"[207] as the transhumanist James Hughes puts it.

We are witnessing an attack on the *truth*. Everything becomes an interpretation to the point of denying the very existence of reality. If you don't have truth, if you don't have roots to draw from, if you don't have firm points, everything slips into the indefinite and everything is fragmented, re-signified and distorted:

> Our sex is more pertinent to our existence in a living biosphere than anything we think. It is our root in the real world. How will we free ourselves from this virtual reality imposed by corporate interests, telling us our sex is not real?[208]

---

[207] James Hugues. 'Democratic Transhumanism 2.0'. 2002. Quoted in Pièces et Main d'Oeuvre. *Manifeste des Chimpanzés du futur contre le transhumanisme*. Grenoble: Service compris. 2017.

[208] Jennifer Bilek. 'Reality Has Become a Tourist Attraction'. 7 December 2022. In *The 11th Hour*. <https://www.the11thhourblog.com/post/reality-has-become-a-tourist-attraction >, accessed 27 April 2023.

The annihilation of truth is ongoing and every time truth is denied prepares the brain to believe the next lie, any lie. In the cybernetic order, algorithms will reveal what will be considered the truth of things and events, eliminating our ability to deal with reality and with the body itself, thus not allowing an understanding of all the possible discomforts, intolerances and problems caused by society towards precisely that body caught in the grip of stereotypes, social pressures, performativity, expectations and rebellion.

The tyrannical algorithmic truth cannot be questioned: who better than the algorithms of artificial intelligence that are preparing to deeply probe our every single gesture and emotion that will reveal to us what our 'gender identity' will be and, for every aspect of our existence, what will be best for us? The individual is uprooted and dissociated from reality in a progressive immersion in a transparent algorithmic cage which will mediate his or her access to reality and which will merge it with fiction and appearance.

The solidity and duration of truth vanishes. Those factual truths that Hannah Arendt considered 'stubborn' give way to the emptying of sense and meaning. Is the era of truth disintegrated, totally over? The truth of our bodies will always resurface, but we just have to ask ourselves if there will be anyone still able to perceive her/his body and fight for it.

All ties to the real, natural world must be severed. Everything must be artificial, synthetic and virtual. Dissociation from our sexed body opens up the erasure of truth and the erasure of our bodies. We go from dissociation with the sexed body to dissociation with reality itself.

As Jennifer Bilek puts it:

These same corporations promoting body dissociation as progressive, telling us they care about the marginalized, are destroying the natural world as they build us synthetic simulacrums and cultivate our acceptance that it is a utopia. In 1965, Monsanto gave us AstroTurf for our lawns, destroyed the integrity of our food, and now we have synthetic sex identities. We are encased in a virtual world we can't see.

I am not making this up. Silicon Valley, in bed with the medical-industrial complex and supported by billionaire bankers, is selling us a singularity, a neuro-linked reality, a metaverse, a virtual reality. They are telling us what they are doing as they are doing it. We are so ensconced in it that we don't know what is real, what we feel, what is the truth, or what is right. Where will we be in ten years?[209]

They are all pieces that must be joined together, a total demolition of the previous forms of existence is underway: how one comes into the world, biological sex, education, relationships, the family, even the diet that is about to become synthetic. There must be no room for what will be deemed obsolete and a hindrance to the imperatives of the techno-scientific system.

The society that emerges is a mere aggregation of individuals that will lead them to want to become independent, will lead

---

[209] Jennifer Bilek. 'Reality Has Become A Tourist Attraction'. 7 December 2022. In *The 11th Hour*. <https://www.the11thhourblog.com/post/reality-has-become-a-tourist-attraction>, accessed 27 April 2023.

them to want to free themselves from the family, from nascent life, from their sexed body, from their own existence, from old age and from death. Free from everything, even from oneself. Instead of feeling dependent on each other and an integral part of a democratic community. Instead of conceiving a sense of freedom that is independent of any written order and that maintains limits and boundaries that cannot be crossed by technocrats.

The goal is a 'liberation' and 'emancipation' from the living itself—spontaneous, autonomous and unpredictable—and from the constraints of nature from which birth also derives with all its uncertainties. The price for emancipation from the living and its natural constraints is *submission* to the technological constraints of the machine world.

The family will be considered an absolute evil; retrograde in its hope to form a single united body with the children. It will be disintegrated by reducing or removing parental authority. If the children no longer have parents, it will be a court and technicians in white coats who will decide what is in the 'best interests of the minor'.

The human being with their own identity and their history is being replaced with a 'neutral' individual who can be whatever she/he—'they'—want by rejecting all limits. The gaze will be moved by a 'we' that unites with the ego, with the subjective will, with one's desire that must become law.

Alongside total commodification of every dimension including nuclear power, a threshold has long been crossed. With genetic engineering and synthetic biology another threshold was crossed. And now we are in the era of the redesignability of the human being.

Transhumanist eugenicist technocrats are increasingly able to intervene in life, death, bodies and the very boundaries of the human with techno-scientific developments that go faster than the public's understanding of their consequences and of the legal regulation that can only follow them. It is no coincidence that these developments are defined as technologies that mark a *deep* and unprecedented transformation of the world and of human beings precisely because they aim to redesign them.

Today, bodies are the new terrain of conquest and battle. A war against bodies being reduced to guinea pigs to be genetically manipulated, against life responsible for having been born and expecting to die, against 'natural' procreation which must become artificial, against nature as the main witness of what life is like outside the artificialisation of the laboratory, with its slow rhythms punctuated by its biological features. The aim is to make a human being a mere appendage that can be dismantled and reassembled continuously in a thousand fluid universes.

In all of this, even the irreducible and inaccessible disappear to leave room only for manipulation. Anything that is not totally decipherable, controllable and harnessable by first mechanistic means and then algorithmic rationality disappears, with the presumption of the rational and technical gaze on the world that aims to bend every manifestation of the living towards itself, for its own use and consumption.

Gender ideology and the whole pharmaceutical, techno-medical and bio-nanotechnological apparatus pave the ground for the normalisation and generalisation of the developments of artificial reproduction techniques and genetic engineering through ad hoc propaganda. As Jennifer Bilek lucidly writes:

> Conjuring medical synthetic sex identities and selling them to the next generation, simultaneously with their sterilization, and tacking them onto a human rights movement of people who are same-sex attracted, when all will need assisted reproductive technology, is not an accident. It is political genius sewn to the gargantuan marketing apparatus of the techno-medical industry.
>
> These modern families are paving the way for a total colonization of human reproduction which is why the current family model is being attacked along with reproductive sex. LGBT Inc.'s tech offspring emerging from these experiments will not be rooted in a set of parental genes but in a factory compilation of genes and bodies involved in their gestation. [...] But now it is amped up by a tech frenzy wedded to unfettered corporatism and the power of what has become the LGBT Inc., a juggernaut of force manifested out of corporatizing sexual attraction and fetishes.[210]

According to some, dealing with surrogacy, gender or the commune of Bibbiano near Bologna is a sign of obtuseness and a desire to divert attention from other more urgent issues. In reality it is from these arguments that the future of our civilisation can

---

210 Jennifer Bilek. 'Is humanity ready for LGBTQ+ tech babies and the full erasure of women from reproduction?' In *Human Events*. <https://humanevents.com/2023/06/11/jennifer-bilek-is-humanity-ready-for-lgbtq-tech-babies-and-the-full-erasure-of-women-from-reproduction>, accessed 06 July 2023.

be guessed.[211] Our sexed roots, the dimension of procreation and, ultimately, humanity—women, children and men—are the last frontier against transhumanism. At stake is the very existence of reality under siege by artificial dismantling and reconstruction.

The river is in full flow! To stop the water before it overwhelms us, we need to find a firm shore: that line of resistance for those of us who are determined to remain anchored to reality, in defence of humanity and in defence of all that is living and not made up of silicon circuits. A wild and free living.

Ours is a race against time, but we absolutely cannot avoid not taking part.

---

211 Francesco Borgonovo. In *Orso Bruno*. 9 June 2023. <https://www.byoblu.com/2023/06/09/orsobruno-9-giugno-2023-francesco-borgonovo/9>, accessed 27 June 2023.

Also available from Spinifex Press

Detransition: Beyond Before and After
Max Robinson

Many feminists are concerned about the way transgender ideology naturalizes patriarchal views of sex stereotypes, and encourages transition as a way of attempting to escape misogyny.

In this brave and thoughtful book, Max Robinson goes beyond the 'before' and 'after' of the transition she underwent and takes us through the processes that led her, first, to transition in an attempt to get relief from her distress, and then to detransition, as she discovered feminist thought and community.

The author makes a case for a world in which all medical interventions for the purpose of assimilation are open to criticism. This book is a far-reaching discussion of women's struggles to survive under patriarchy, which draws upon a legacy of radical and lesbian feminist ideas to arrive at conclusions.

Robinson's bold discussion of both transition and detransition is meant to provoke a much-needed conversation about who benefits from transgender medicine and who has to bear the hidden cost of these interventions.

ISBN 9781925950403

Now available as Audiobook
ISBN 9781925950786, Length 4h 31m

*If you would like to know more about
Spinifex Press, write to us for a free catalogue, visit our
website or email us for further information
on how to subscribe to our monthly newsletter.*

Spinifex Press
PO Box 105
Mission Beach QLD 4852
Australia
www.spinifexpress.com.au
women@spinifexpress.com.au